McMaster Journal of Theology and Ministry
ISSN 1481–0794

Editor
John J. H. Lee

McMaster Divinity College

1280 Main Street West
Hamilton, Ontario, Canada L8S 4K1
email: mjtm@mcmaster.ca

McMaster Journal of Theology and Ministry is an electronic and print journal of McMaster Divinity College, in Hamilton, Ontario, Canada. It seeks to provide pastors, educators, and interested lay persons with the fruits of theological, biblical, and professional studies in an accessible form. It succeeds the Divinity College's former periodicals, the *Theological Bulletin*, *Theodolite*, and the *McMaster Journal of Theology*. Each volume covers an academic year (September to August). Reviews and articles are posted on the *MJTM* website at:

https://mcmasterdivinity.ca/mjtm

and beginning with Volume Nine (2007–2008), the volume is available in hard copy as well.

The *McMaster Journal of Theology and Ministry* is also available on the EBSCO database, and abstracts are included in Religious and Theological Abstracts (RTA).

Manuscripts, books for review, and communications should be addressed to the Editor through the email address on the journal website. Contributors are encouraged to use the style of McMaster Divinity College, available at:

https://mcmasterdivinity.ca/resources-forms/mdc-style-guide

All articles and book reviews are peer-reviewed for appropriate academic and professional standards. Special thanks to D. S. Martin for selecting and editing the poetry.

Copies of the printed version can be ordered from Wipf and Stock Publishers in Eugene, OR (USA) through their website wipfandstock.com. Copies are also available through the McMaster Divinity College bookshop (books@readon.ca).

Content of the *McMaster Journal of Theology and Ministry* is copyright by McMaster Divinity College.

For more information about McMaster Divinity College, please visit the College's website at mcmasterdivinity.ca.

Back cover artwork: *Shot Pillars* (Sculpture by Romanian artist Liviu Mocan; 2003)

The artist's website: https://www.liviumocan.ro

Neighbourly Love in Genesis 2:18–25: The Root of the Second Great Commandment

Aaron K. Husband[1]
InterVarsity Campus Minister, Concordia University, Montreal, QC, Canada

To love one's neighbour as oneself, matching closely Lev 19:18b, is one of the two great commands (Matt 22:34–40). Jesus says, "[a]ll the Law and the Prophets hang on these two commandments." (Matt 22:40, NIV) However, as an individual text, Lev 19:18 is hardly a prominent verse. Henry Kelly even writes, "[i]t is not only not prominent, it is the very opposite of prominent."[2] Still, as Kelly exhibits, it is clear that Jesus and the New Testament authors considered neighbourly love as foundational to Old Testament ethics (e.g., Rom 13:8–10; Gal 5:14; Luke 6:27–36; 10:25–37; 1 John 4:11).[3] It is not uncommon for Old Testament quotations in the New Testament to serve as allusions to broader principles or theological concepts.[4] Often, the individually cited passages are quotable expressions of the principle or allusions to contexts where that principle is recognizable. Given Lev 19:18's lack of prominence and granting that

---

1. Many thanks to the MJTM team for their valuable comments and support as well as Dr. Ashley Hibbard for her helpful remarks and encouraging words.
2. Kelly, "Love of Neighbor," 267.
3. See Kelly, "Love of Neighbor," 274–79.
4. For example, Matt 2:18 quotes Jer 31:15 after Herod's genocide. Though the exact quote speaks to the grief of God's people, the context is a declaration of hope amidst immense tragedy and suffering, making clear that God is bringing his salvation through the worst of circumstances, a theme that is prominent in stories like the Flood or the Exodus.

Jesus and the apostles understood the Old Testament as designed, this is almost certainly the situation.[5]

If there is a foundational Old Testament law of neighbourly love rooted in broader principles, one would expect to find it in Gen 2:18–25. However, the love of neighbour is rarely considered central to the scene. Rather, commentary is frequently limited to its importance for marriage.[6] The text's relevance to marriage is no doubt correct, as made clear by the narrator in Gen 2:24 and confirmed by both Jesus (Matt 19:3–9) and Paul (Eph 5:25–33). However, the chief purpose of this essay is to contend that Gen 2:18–25 establishes an ethic of neighbourly love, concluding with brief reflections on the implications for friendship and the lives of those who are single.

After briefly reviewing why Lev 19:18 in itself is unlikely to be the second great command, four mutually reinforcing propositions will be defended to argue for neighbourly love in Gen 2:18–25: (1) Gen 1–2's idyllic nature lends credence to the passage's societal implications; (2) the interrelated elements of Gen 2:17–18 imply a need for, and call to, universal, neighbourly love; (3) Gen 2:23's body language establishes a covenantal value of loving one's neighbour as oneself, and (4) both the Old Testament and New Testament refer to the scene in non-marital contexts suggesting the text serves to establish neighbourly love.

Neighbourly Love Summing the Law

From a grammatical-historical standpoint, Lev 19:18 as an isolated command cannot bear the weight of the New Testament's emphasis. As Kelly defends well, "[o]nce the importance of love

---

5. On New Testament authors' understanding the Old Testament as designed, see Pickup, "New Testament Interpretation."

6. For example, Andrew Steinmann comments that the text "defines marriage as God's establishment for the proper relationship of the two sexes to each other" (*Genesis*, 67). Gordon Wenham says, "Here the ideal of marriage as it was understood in ancient Israel is being portrayed, a relationship characterized by harmony and intimacy between the partners" (*Genesis 1–15*, 69). See also Waltke, *Genesis*, 90; von Rad, *Genesis*, 82.

was realized, the Levitical verse was emancipated from its narrow limits and elevated to a place of honor."[7]

The whole verse reads, "[d]o not seek revenge or bear a grudge against anyone among your people, but love your neighbor as yourself. I am the LORD." (Lev 19:18, NIV) The entire law can hardly be hung on not being resentful towards one's people. Loving as oneself does reappear later (vv. 33–34), applying it to foreigners as well (cf. Deut 10:17–19). Still, though this hints at a universalized love ethic, it is difficult to see it as the foundation for it.

Though some suggest love could be central to the holiness laws of Lev 18–20,[8] the context of the verse gives little hope for it summing the whole of Old Testament ethics, surrounded by a variety of Decalogic, ceremonial, and other miscellaneous laws.[9] Further, the broader literary structure of Leviticus does not highlight Lev 19:18 but emphasizes the atonement rituals.[10] Indeed, the title the NIV gives the chapter sums up the verse's prominence: "Various Laws."

However, much like answers to once confusing riddles, that love should summarize all Old Testament ethical instruction is intuitive, at least after it is pointed out as Paul does in Rom 13:8–10. He quotes much of the Decalogue pertaining to the treatment of others and says the love of neighbour both sums and fulfills these and all other commands. For Paul, lived love is the value summarizing the covenant as expressed in the values of the Decalogue, the "tablets of the covenant" (Deut 9:11, NIV).

Shortly after the Decalogue, Exod 21–23 shows concrete examples of love in specific situations before the covenant is affirmed in Exod 24. Similarly, the Shema comes immediately following the restatement of the Decalogue in Deuteronomy, and a justification for keeping God's commands is repeatedly "so it will go well" for them and those around them (e.g., Deut 5:16,

---

7. Kelly, "Love of Neighbor," 280.
8. E.g., Morales, *Who Shall Ascend the Mountain of the Lord?* 207–13.
9. For a summary of Lev 19:18's immediate context, see Kelly, "Love of Neighbor," 267–69.
10. See Morales, *Who Shall Ascend the Mountain of the Lord?* 23–38.

29; 6:3, 18; 8:16; 12:25, 28). After Moses recounts the remaking of the tablets, he summarizes, "[a]nd now, Israel, what does the LORD your God ask of you but to fear the LORD your God, to walk in obedience to him, to love him, to serve the LORD your God with all your heart and with all your soul, and to observe the LORD's commands and decrees that I am giving you today *for your own good*?" (Deut 10:12–13, NIV; emphasis mine). Echoes of the Shema are clear in v. 12, and, in v. 13, the goodness or wellness of the people is a key purpose of observing God's laws, which are the ways of living according to the covenant expressed by the Decalogue. This implies keeping God's commands is for the good of oneself and those around them. In other words, "[l]ove does no harm to a neighbor. Therefore love is the fulfillment of the law" (Rom 13:10, NIV).

Paul regularly saw the values underlying laws (e.g., 1 Cor 9:8–12). The laws are concrete, paradigmatic expressions of values in their context. To Jesus and Paul, these values are loving God and neighbours. It is the value of neighbourly love, *most quotable* in Lev 19:18, that, along with loving God, all the Law and Prophets hang on. The true root of this value, however, is Gen 2:18–25, as will be argued below.

Proposition 1: Genesis 1–2 as Idyllic

In the epic of the biblical plot, Gen 1–2 describes an idyllic state where the line between heaven and earth is blurred. This is recognizable once Eden is seen as a temple sanctuary. Genesis 1–2 presenting creation as a tabernacle or temple has been extensively documented and is widely held amongst scholars.[11] In his book on the biblical theology of Leviticus, L. Michael Morales summarizes:

> the early chapters of Genesis were not composed merely to rehearse origins, but to inform the worship of ancient Israel, explaining the

---

11. See especially Beale, "Eden"; Davidson, "Earth's First Sanctuary." Other examples include Hamilton, *Book of Genesis*, 210; Hinckley, "Adam"; Morales, *Who Shall Ascend the Mountain of the Lord?* 39–74; Sailhamer, *Pentateuch*, 99; Wenham, *Genesis 1–15*, 90; Waltke, *Genesis*, 85.

rituals of the tabernacle cultus. Genesis 1–3 conforms to the general priestly categories of sacred space (the cosmos as a tabernacle, Eden as the holy of holies), sacred time (the Sabbath) and sacred status (Adam's priestly role), all of which will inform our understanding of the tabernacle cultus.[12]

Much more is being established, however. Humanity is called to both fill and subdue the earth (Gen 1:26–28) and to work and keep the Garden (Gen 2:15). Gregory Beale argues persuasively that this implies humanity's role is to extend the Garden-Temple to all the earth:

> The intention seems to be that Adam was to widen the boundaries of the Garden in ever increasing circles by extending the order of the garden sanctuary into the inhospitable outer spaces. The outward expansion would include the goal of spreading the glorious presence of God. This would occur especially by Adam's progeny born in his image and thus reflecting God's image and the light of his presence, as they continued to obey the mandate given to their parents and went out to subdue the outer country until the Eden sanctuary covered the earth.[13]

Genesis 1–2, then, describes a state in the presence of God designed for God's vice-regents, humanity (Gen 1:26–28),[14] to continue God's creative work by spreading his heavenliness throughout the earth. Therefore, it would be natural for it to be showing, and implicitly commanding, an idyllic ethic which all the Law and the Prophets hang on. Indeed, it is perfectly appropriate to consider narrative as law or instruction. As Gordon Wenham says, "[t]he narratives in Genesis teach ethics and theology just as much as do laws and theological sermons found elsewhere in the Pentateuch, and for this reason these also belong to the Torah."[15]

A hint at the ethical role Gen 1–2 plays is found in Matt 19:3–9. Jesus appeals to both Gen 1:27 and 2:24 as trumping the later

---

12. Morales, *Who Shall Ascend the Mountain of the Lord?* 53.
13. Beale, "Eden," 11.
14. See Middleton "Image of God"; Clines, "Image of God." See especially Middleton, *Liberating Image*.
15. Wenham, *Genesis 1–15*, 5.

allowance of divorce certificates, noting that "it was not this way from the beginning." (Matt 19:8b, NIV). Because of the standard set narratively by the pre-sin texts, Jesus recognized divorce certificates were only a practice of harm reduction. As R. T. France puts it:

> Jesus therefore refuses to allow a necessary concession to human sinfulness to be elevated into a divine principle. The ideal is rather to be found in going back to first principles, to what was in the beginning . . . Jesus' appeal to first principles has the effect of apparently setting one passage of Scripture against another, but this is not in the sense of repudiating one in favour of the other, but of insisting that each is given its proper function, the one as a statement of the ideal will of God, the other as a (regrettable but necessary) provision for those occasions when human sinfulness has failed to maintain the ideal.[16]

Genesis 2:18–25 reflects the ethical ideal. Not only that, but it is the only story in the biblical narrative of humans interacting within the ideal prior to the ruin of sin. It should be expected for neighbourly love to be a first principle found there.

Proposition 2: Genesis 2:17–18 and Neighbourly Love

Moving to the text itself opens a veritable floodgate of famously debated, interrelated topics, including the significance of the Tree of the Knowledge of Good and Evil, the precise problem that aloneness presents, and the meaning of עזר כנגדו, among others. These debates will be briefly waded into so a cumulative case can be made for Gen 2:18–25's import to neighbourly love. In short, the Tree of the Knowledge of Good and Evil, the problem of solitude, and the solution of help are neither gendered nor unique to marriage. The text displays a marriage in the context of the general need for robust, faithful friendship and community—pivotal to marriage but not unique to it—and readers are to see Adam and Eve as both an archetypal couple and archetypal neighbours.

---

16. France, *Matthew*, 284.

The Tree of the Knowledge of Good and Bad
As the scene begins immediately following the prohibition against the fruit from the Tree of the Knowledge of Good and Evil, understanding the tree's function will be beneficial.[17]

As for good and evil (טוב and רע), each has a range of meanings beyond moral good and evil. Morality can be in view (e.g., Ps 14:1; 140:1–2) but also the generally positive, pleasant, or beneficial and the generally negative, unpleasant, or harmful (e.g., Lev 27:10; Josh 23:15; 2 Kgs 2:19; Jer 24:2).

Together, the phrase טוב ורע ("good and evil") is a common Hebrew merism. John Walton categorizes its usages by the verbs used with it, giving four categories.[18] First, when used with speaking (e.g., Gen 24:50), "good and evil" suggest that the speaker pass judgment, issue a decision, or, when negated, to not do so. Secondly, when used with hearing, it means to listen with discernment (e.g., 2 Sam 14:17). Thirdly, when used with knowing or its synonyms coupled with prepositions, it refers to the capacity to be discriminating, discerning what is in their or others' best interests. There are only three occurrences from this category in the Old Testament. They associate lacking knowing good and evil with a childlike state (Isa 7:15–16), an inexperienced state also compared to childhood (1 Kgs 3:7–9) or being too elderly to discern wisely (2 Sam 19:35). Finally, there is one instance, outside of Gen 2–3, that uses the merism with knowing but without prepositions (Deut 1:39). There, it is also speaking of children, referring to their inability to be discriminating, make decisions, or live independently. Walton goes on to say, "[t]he common denominator of these references is 'discernment or discriminating wisdom.'"[19]

Though there are only four Old Testament passages after Gen 2–3 related to knowing good and evil, three link the idea to being like a child, lacking wisdom, and it is no stretch to think the way

---

17. For a summary of viewpoints on the trees, see Wallace, "Tree of Knowledge."
18. Walton, *Genesis*, 171.
19. Walton, *Genesis*, 171.

in which the elderly come to lack discernment is a return to childlike dependency. It is, therefore, a reasonable inference to think lacking the knowledge of good and evil is to be like a child, lacking wisdom.[20]

As such, it is most likely that the tree represents wisdom in a full sense, relating to wellbeing, pleasantness, and morality, though it is too far to say taking the fruit was a grasp for omniscience. Just as children must learn not only to choose good over evil, but also general, healthy communal and individual functioning, humanity needs to trust God for wisdom in and for all things.

Given this understanding, it is most likely that humanity was to gain the knowledge of good and evil, growing up into wisdom. It is surely true that women and men would need to know what is good and bad in their governance of the creatures (Gen 1:26–28; 2:19–20). Additionally, to be able to discern good and evil is roundly positive in the remainder of the Old Testament. Contrary to popular caricatures, the tree was no trick or trap, but a gift. God created the Tree of the Knowledge of Good and Evil for humanity to gain the knowledge of good and evil; that is, to gain wisdom.

Yet the tree was prohibited. Some believe the fruit was barred only temporarily, and the first sin was to take it prematurely.[21] However, as Peterson says, "[t]he syntax of the sentence (negation לא plus the imperfect verb) is a permanent prohibition. They were never to partake of the tree."[22] Rather, as argued by Keil and Delitzsch, God wished for humanity to gain the knowledge of good and evil by means of *not taking* the fruit, gaining it through trusting him instead.[23] Note that it is the *Tree* of the Knowledge of Good and Evil, not the *Fruit* of the Knowledge of Good and Evil; the tree could very well impart wisdom, via the

---

20. See also Buchanan, "Old Testament Meaning."
21. E.g., Provan, *Discovering Genesis*, 73–75. See also Provan, *Seriously Dangerous Religion*, 112–15.
22. Peterson, *Genesis*, 43. Likewise, see Wenham, *Genesis 1–15*, 67–68.
23. See Keil and Delitzsch, *Biblical Commentary*, 86.

LORD, apart from its fruit.[24] Therefore, the tree's existence itself need not imply the fruit was to be eaten, as is sometimes suggested.[25] The plot tension is not whether humans should gain wisdom, but *how* they will gain wisdom. Will they trust God for his wisdom (cf. Ps 111:10; Prov 1:7; 2:6; 11:30; Jas 1:5–8), or take it for themselves?

Eventually, after perceiving the fruit as desirable for gaining wisdom (Gen 3:6), the humans take the knowledge of good and evil. Now having wisdom, they are like God in a tragic new way (Gen 3:22; cf. 1:26). That said, humanity having wisdom is best understood as a half-truth, underscoring the serpent's crafty deception (Gen 3:4–5), for it is not God's true wisdom imparted, but their own wisdom taken. Claiming what could awkwardly be called "wisdom autonomy," humanity and God now both share similar, though rival, self-understandings as to their authoritative status to pronounce what is wise. Indeed, the woman saw that the fruit was good (Gen 3:6), taking the role of God, who saw what was good seven times in Gen 1. This human pride and pseudo-wisdom will only lead to exile and death (Gen 2:17; 3:22–24).

Aloneness and Help
Immediately following the risk of death apart from obedience, Gen 2:18 establishes a plot tension: it is not good that the human is alone. Commentators are varied regarding the precise problem solitude presents. Iain Provan thinks it is related to humanity's vocation—rulership (Gen 1:26–28) and the priestly gardening duties (Gen 2:15)—writing that, without community, the strength of the first human is insufficient for these tasks.[26] Others (e.g., D. J. A. Clines) believe the problem is procreation. Man needs woman to produce children, and he asserts woman is no help regarding ruling or gardening.[27] Alternatively, Wenham

---

24. Compare the Tree of Life imparting healing through its leaves, not only its fruit (Rev 22:2).
25. E.g., Provan, *Discovering Genesis*, 73–75; Eiselen, "Tree of the Knowledge," 106.
26. Provan, *Discovering Genesis*, 77.
27. Clines, *What Does Eve Do to Help?* 34–35.

proposes, "[t]he help looked for is not just assistance in his daily work or in the procreation of children, though these aspects may be included, but the mutual support companionship provides."[28]

Here, a much narrower understanding shall be offered, though the result can hold the core principles from the views above simultaneously. As this plot tension follows immediately after the forbidden fruit, the problem of aloneness is most likely to be understood considering the preceding verse. The human, when alone, would tend towards eating the fruit, taking wisdom autonomy, choosing death. Humans need communal help not to.

As the solution to a problem is to solve the problem, this view can be tested by a study of the solution: a "helper" (עזר).[29] Space does not permit a robust word study, but a brief review of the noun's twenty-one Old Testament occurrences shall show that rescue or support against death is well within the term's possible undertones.[30] Indeed, there is remarkable consistency towards that end. Although a word in any given context can be used in a unique sense, it is perfectly plausible for help in Gen 2 to carry this nuance, as Gen 2:17 notes a risk of death.

Only three instances of עזר outside Gen 2 do not refer to God (Isa 30:5; Ezek 2:14; Dan 11:34). None of these refer to women, procreation, or marriage, but are military in nature. Indeed, most occurrences of עזר picture God as military help (e.g., "and the other [son of Moses] was named Eliezer, for he said, 'My father's God was my helper; he saved me from the sword of Pharoah'" [Exod 18:4, NIV]). Of note is the connection of עזר with shields found in Deut 33:26–29; Ps 33:20; 89:18–19; Ps 115:9–11:

> O house of Israel, trust in the LORD—
>   he is their help and shield.
> O house of Aaron, trust in the LORD —

---

28. Wenham, *Genesis 1–15*, 68. See also von Rad, *Genesis*, 80.
29. For more on עזר, see Bergmann, "עזר"; Hawkins, "Help"; Koehler and Baumgartner, "עֵזֶר"; Lipiński, "עֵזֶר"; Renn, ed., *Expository Dictionary*, 486.
30. See Hamilton (*Book of Genesis*, 176), who writes, "the verb behind ʿēzer is ʿāzar, which means 'succor,' 'save from danger,' '*deliver from death*.' The woman in Gen 2 delivers or saves man from his solitude" (emphasis mine).

> he is their help and shield.
> You who fear him, trust in the LORD —
> he is their help and shield.

Whether a reinforcing army or a military official, military help, at its most basic, keeps allies from death. The image of shields continues this anti-death theme, as well as such Psalms containing עזר as Ps 70, 121, and 124. In Ps 70, there are those who would wish to take the psalmist's life (Ps 70:2), but the LORD is his help and deliverer (Ps 70:5). Psalm 121 affirms the LORD, the helper coming down the hillside like a reinforcing army (Ps 121:1–2), watches over the lives of his people, keeping them from harm (Ps 121:7). In Ps 124, if God, in whose name Israel finds their help (Ps 124:8), is not on their side, they would be swallowed alive (Ps 124:2–3).

It is similar in Ps 20 and 146. Psalm 20 speaks of the help as military given the mention of military banners (Ps 20:5), alongside horses and chariots (Ps 20:7). Because the help is in a military context, its usage is consistent with an anti-death connotation. Similarly, Ps 146 explores life and death, and mentions God's help directly after the inevitable deaths of untrustworthy humans, offering the psalmist robust hope (Ps 146:2–5).

Indeed, in nearly every usage of עזר in Scripture, the helper either has, explicitly or implicitly, rescued from death, is called upon to do so, or there is a declaration of God as helper in contexts where life and death are juxtaposed. Although, again, any one context can use a word distinctly, this is remarkable consistency, and Gen 2 fits this model well with the juxtaposition of the trees of life and death. Coupled with the simple observation that the problem of solitude is expressed immediately following the trees, naturally connecting them, it is most probable that humans cannot be alone because they need shields: communal help to not take the prohibited fruit, claiming wisdom autonomy.[31] This makes good sense within Gen 2 itself but is also the most

---

31. עזר as anti-death in Gen 2 accords well with R. E. Freidman's translation of עזר כנגדו as "strength corresponding to him," though it arguably loses the elements of assistance and companionship (see Friedman, *Commentary*, 19).

expected understanding of עזר after surveying its scriptural usages.

It is often claimed that women are men's helpers or, at least, a wife is a husband's helper. Certainly, the woman is the first example of a human helper or, perhaps, the first human to be God's means of being a helper, as humans, male and female, are to be his delegated representatives on earth (Gen 1:26–28). However, the nature of עזר as a counter to taking from the tree resists a sex-specific understanding. Indeed, that the עזר turned out to be a woman was probably a shocking twist, especially since military help would not normally be applied to women and "the extant literature of the ancient Near East has preserved no other account of the creation of primordial woman."[32] Humans are humans' helpers—"even women!" an ancient, patriarchal reader could be imagined saying—for it is not good for all humans, regardless of sex, to be alone, and all humans, regardless of sex, tend to take the knowledge of good and evil, claiming wisdom apart from God, seeing for themselves what is good.[33]

Adam as Archetype

Adam's archetypal nature reinforces a gender-neutral understanding of Gen 2:18 and, thus, a non-marital application. Borrowing from Walton, an archetype "refers to a representative of a group in whom all others in the group are embodied. As a result, all members of the group are included and participate with their representative."[34] This function flows naturally from Adam's eventual name, אדם; that is, Human. Walton, affirming Adam and Eve were historical persons, reports the Hebrew language did not exist until the second millennium BCE. Therefore, Adam and Eve would not have spoken Hebrew or called each other by

---

32. Sarna, *Genesis*, 21.
33. Comparably, Sarah Moore Grimké (1792–1873) took the need for a helpmeet to apply, not just to married couples, but to all men and women as equals, though she believed women are men's helpmeet (Taylor and Weir, *Let her Speak for Herself*, 42–46).
34. Walton, *Lost World of Adam and Eve*, 240.

those names. Instead, their names were assigned to them for interpretive purposes.[35]

The remainder of Scripture confirms Adam's archetypal purpose, easily inferable from his eventual name. Adam is used archetypally for both men *and women* in Rom 5 and 1 Cor 15.[36] Although Adam is the only character in the Bible formed of dust (Gen 2:7), Abraham, David, and Job all affirm either themselves or humanity are also of dust (Gen 18:27; Ps 103:14; Job 10:9; 34:15). Similarly, Adam's naming of the animals is most probably a picture of the gender-neutral image of God, showing humanity's royal authority and imitating God's naming from Gen 1.[37] Of course, Adam's freedoms and prohibitions regarding the trees (Gen 2:16–17) also applied to the woman (Gen 3:2–3), again reinforcing his generally non-gendered archetypal function.

Adam's non-gendered function includes his priestly duties of working and keeping the Garden (Gen 2:15).[38] This is inferable from the other ways Adam is an archetype for women, but also the image of God and the work of Gen 1:26–28, alongside simple practicality in a garden sanctuary. Furthermore, as the biblical plot continues, the whole nation of Israel was called to fulfill this work, the spreading of God's Garden-Temple as a kingdom of priests (Exod 19:6; cf. Isa 42:6; 49:6). The kingdom of priests, Adam's task to spread the Garden over all the world, included the women. That women were not priests in Israel is not a challenge to this hypothesis, just as it could not be argued any non-priestly male is not archetypally represented by Adam. Eventually, this image begins to be fulfilled in the church, male and female (see 1 Pet 2:9; Rev 1:4–6; 5:9–10; 20:6; 22:1–5).[39] Women being included when the priestly theme of working and keeping fully flowers in the biblical plotline suggests women were in-

---

35. Walton, *Lost World of Adam and Eve*, 58–59.
36. He is also used in other ways (see Walton, *Lost World of Adam and Eve*, 92–95).
37. See Davidson, *Genesis 1–11*, 37; Hamilton, *Book of Genesis*, 176; Middleton "Image of God"; Steinmann, *Genesis*, 67.
38. See Walton, *Genesis*, 172–74.
39. For more on this fulfillment, see Beale, "Eden."

cluded in the tasks of Gen 2:15. As a result, everything God pronounces to Adam in Gen 3:17–19 applies to women, highlighting his typically gender-neutral archetypal function.

Even more, the common noun אדם either refers collectively to humanity or an individual human.[40] Like English's "humanity" or "human," both usages are gender neutral. The term is grammatically masculine and therefore calls for grammatically masculine pronouns, but this is only a grammatical construction.[41] Further, the proper name "Adam" most likely does not appear until Gen 4:25 in the original text.[42] In short, there are no definite indicators of Adam's sex until Gen 2:23, when the term for a male human (איש) is used.[43] Not only does the ambiguity at Gen 2:18 (and 2:15) directly reinforce a gender-neutral understanding,[44] it again highlights Adam's generally non-gendered archetypal function.

That Adam is continually described simply as the human, eventually named Human, is used archetypally throughout Scripture for all humans regardless of sex, and the lack of knowledge of his sex until Gen 2:23 all reinforce Gen 2:18 should be understood in a gender-neutral light. Though help should certainly be a part of marriage, humans need humans to help them choose life, as Moses did: "I have set before you life and death, blessings and curses. Now choose life, so that you and your children may live and that you may love the Lord your God, listen to his voice, and hold fast to him." (Deut 30:19b–20a, NIV).

---

40. On אדם, see Hendel, "Adam," 18–19; Koehler and Baumgartner, "אָדָם," 14; Maass, "אָדָם"; McKenzie, *Dictionary*, 12; Motyer, "Adam"; Wallace, "Adam"; Westermann, "אָדָם," 31–42.

41. See Steins, "Grammar"; Hess, "Adam."

42. See Lussier, "Adam"; Maass, "אָדָם," 79; McKenzie, *Dictionary*, 12; Wallace, "Adam," 62–63; Westermann, "אָדָם," 34.

43. This is not to say Adam was not a male (Gen 1:27; 2:22–23) (see Hamilton, *Book of Genesis*, 177–78). Rather, the storyteller has intentionally and strategically not revealed his sex for interpretively significant reasons.

44. Hendel agrees (see "Adam," 18).

Genesis 2:25, ערום, and Final Thoughts on Genesis 2:17–18

Genesis 2:25 provides further support for understanding Gen 2:18 to be outlining humanity's need for, and call to be, deeply enriching community. In the closing verse of the scene,[45] there are no children, no description of working and keeping the Garden, and no interaction with the animals, as would be expected if these are the direct problems associated with solitude. Because the one-flesh relationship that Gen 2:24 describes is a narrator's commentary,[46] there is not even any indication of intercourse between the first couple.[47] Rather, the scene closes with the two naked, a sign of "openness and trust,"[48] and without shame. The solution to the problem is, thus far, successful. They have not taken fruit from the Tree of the Knowledge of Good and Evil and therefore have no reason for shame, resulting in a well-rounded plot for Gen 2:18–25.

The nakedness could be viewed as something unique to marriage. However, there are several reasons to view this as a picture of the ideal for all humans, in addition to it aligning with previously argued plot points. First, at this stage of the plot, this is either all of humanity or the representatives of all of humanity. Therefore, the picture *is* of all humanity naked and without shame together. Secondly, both Gen 2:25 and Gen 3:6–8 associate nakedness with shamelessness and being clothed with covering shame. Within the immediate plot, sexual intimacy is not the image nakedness procures, but innocence and honour.[49] Thirdly, since the phrase "the knowledge of good and evil" suggests an initial childlike state for humanity, it would be more narratively congruent for the depiction of nakedness to also be a childlike state, frolicking freely, unashamed.[50] The Eden story is a move-

---

45. Though Gen 2:25 pivots the plot to Gen 3, it primarily closes the previous section, contra Turner-Smith, "Naked."
46. See Tosato, "On Genesis 2:24."
47. This does not necessarily mean they did not have sex, merely that this is not the focus of the narrative.
48. Waltke, *Genesis*, 90.
49. See Davidson, *Genesis 1–11*, 38; von Rad, *Genesis*, 83.
50. Wenham agrees by saying, "[t]hey were like young children unashamed of their nakedness" (*Genesis 1–15*, 71).

ment from childlike innocence to childlike folly. Fourth, Jesus instructed to become like a child (Matt 18:3) and emphasized the fatherhood of God (e.g., Matt 6:9; Luke 15:11–32), a theme prominent in the New Testament (e.g., Rom 8:16–17; 1 John 3:1). That Jesus and the New Testament authors recognized a childlike state—being born again (John 3:3)—was an Eden-like, New Creation state would be unsurprising.

Some may suggest the oft-debated qualifier for the help (כנגדו) relates to the relationship between women and men, and therefore Gen 2:18 cannot be gender neutral. However, confident claims from the clause alone, other than the most general, outstrip the evidence available. Walton says its "profile leaves so much room that it is useless for giving us direction."[51] He even candidly writes, "[t]he best procedure from a methodological standpoint in this kind of situation is to find something sufficiently vague to cover the territory."[52] The phrase עזר כנגדו boasts a vast array of translations, including "a helper suitable for him" (NIV, NASB), "a helper fit for him" (ESV, RSV), "a companion for him who corresponds to him" (NET), "helper—as his counterpart" (YLT), "a helper as his partner" (NRSVue), "a helper who is just right for him"(NLT), and "a helper that is perfect for him" (CEB). Woodenly, כנגדו could be rendered "as in front of him (according to what is in front of him)"[53] or "like opposite him."[54] As Provan says, "That is: the help must be both similar to the earthling ('like' him) and yet also different from him ('opposite, over against, at a distance from him')."[55] This is, indeed, rather vague.

Considering the context set by the observations and arguments above, and other supporting texts soon to be observed, it is unlikely the difference envisioned by כנגדו is the sexes per se. Rather, the human needs another human with different giftings. Other humans, whether male or female, are necessarily different

---

51. Walton, *Genesis*, 176.
52. Walton, *Genesis*, 177.
53. Hamilton, *Book of Genesis*, 175.
54. Wenham, *Genesis 1–15*, 68; Provan, *Discovering Genesis*, 78.
55. Provan, *Discovering Genesis*, 78.

in at least some senses. An animal, among which there was not an עזר כנגדו, could very well offer limited companionship or even save someone's life, but they would not be like opposite him. That is, they would not be a mirror image; a different human endowed with the richness God has endowed the first human, yet gifted in other ways, so that together they may have life to the full and be robust rescue for each other.[56]

Indeed, this view makes the greatest sense of the animal parade. That the parade is the first event following the establishment of solitude as a plot tension and that an עזר was not found among the other creatures (Gen 2:20) highlights they were considered a possible solution to the problem of aloneness, at least by the human. However, Gen 1 notes *ten times* that creatures reproduce according to their kind. It would be odd that God would want Adam to consider bestiality, even if only to reject it. Some solve the puzzle by arguing it was for Adam to become aware of his own loneliness.[57] This is likely correct, but even so, the animals failing to be the loving companions that call humans to faithfulness is a more natural fit in the plot, including if God's two stage process is partly for Adam's ability to recognize his loneliness for himself. Indeed, even the married and sexually active can be lonely and still in need of help.

A paraphrase of עזר כנגדו worthy of consideration is "a strengthening companion as a mirror image of him." Though it is difficult to translate עזר to make the connection with the forbidden fruit explicit, this captures key elements of the phrase and would draw English readers' minds back to the image of God, something עזר כנגדו and the scene is surely intended to do. This, of course, would still be a radical claim about women and their equality to men, jointly made in the image of God. Reflections

---

56. Some may question the gender-neutrality of Gen 2:18 based on 1 Cor 11:9. For the best explanation of 1 Cor 11:2–16, see Peppiatt, *Women*. Her arguments that 1 Cor 11:4–5, 7–10; 14:21–22, 33b–35 refer to Corinthian positions that Paul is refuting are convincing and bolstered by the arguments presented herein. If 1 Cor 11:9 does reflect Paul's view, most likely Paul would be referring to Eve as the *first* helper.

57. See Davidson, *Genesis 1–11*, 37; Wenham, *Genesis 1–15*, 68; von Rad, *Genesis*, 81.

upon the כנגדו (or כנגדה) relationship between men and women need not be hindered by this take. However, the above paraphrase captures how it can apply to any other human as well.

The widely applicable need for help and calling to be helpers naturally lead to neighbourly love. An עזר in the Gen 2 sense simply *is* someone who loves their neighbour as themselves—as bone of their bone and flesh of their flesh—helping others choose life in the most profound sense, acting like Jesus, who came to bring life, and to the full (John 10:10).

Proposition 3: Genesis 2:23 as Covenantal, Neighbourly Love

When this strengthening companion as a mirror image of Adam finally arrives, he declares—with the only pre-sin sentence uttered between humans—that she is his own bone and flesh. Comparable declarations can be found in Gen 29:14; Judg 9:2; 2 Sam 5:1; 1 Chr 11:1; and 2 Sam 19:12–13. In every instance, it is a statement of kinship, though this can range from extended family to tribe or nation. The phrase never refers to the unique relationship between males and females elsewhere in Scripture. The point is easy to ascertain: one can say the other is themselves since they share a body. Coupled with the biblical narrative painting all humans as ultimately one family (e.g., Gen 10; Acts 17:26)—sharing bone and flesh—loving another as oneself is a simple inference. Other humans are family, sharing bodies, so love them that way.

As expected from a creation story, the familial image in Gen 2:23 doubtlessly serves as the narrative foundation for much of the familial language in both the Old Testament and New Testament. In countless laws, the people of Israel are referred to as siblings (e.g., Lev 19:17; 25:35; Deut 15:11; 22:1–4), as are God's people in the New Testament (e.g., Gal 5:13; Heb 3:1; Jas 2:1; 2 Pet 1:10; 1 John 3:14). Within God's covenant community—those who are to most approximate God's ideal in their contexts—people are bone of bone and flesh of flesh.

Interestingly, every Old Testament story containing a person or party declaring another as their bone and flesh eventually results in an agreement or covenant.[58] Therefore, on one level, Gen 2:23 can be seen as the husband's marriage vow, to love his wife as his own body. However, it also likely establishes the covenantal kinship relationships demanded by the law, which is summarized by love. Further, as Adam and Eve either represent all of humanity or are all of humanity, it suggests that there is, or ought to be, a universal covenant to love one another as each loves themselves, precisely what is expected given the role of Gen 1–2 as an idyllic picture, the meaning of Gen 2:17–18, and love summing the law. Loving another as oneself flows naturally from sharing bone and flesh, marking each in covenant kinship with their neighbour, as helpers.

Proposition 4: Reinforcing Texts in the Old and New Testaments

The Old Testament itself refers to Gen 2:18–25 in non-marital contexts. For example, when Boaz praises Ruth, he notes that she left her father and her mother (Ruth 2:11–12), a clear allusion to Gen 2:24, reinforcing the more subtle reference when Ruth chose to hold fast (דבק) to Naomi (Ruth 1:14), the same verb used in Gen 2:24.[59]

Remarkably, Ruth and Naomi's relationship is the only human relationship the Old Testament directly references Gen 2:24 to mark it as being demonstrated in the relationship. Clearly, readers are not supposed to refer to Ruth and Naomi as married. The text marks them as being in-laws (Ruth 1:8–18, 22), Ruth marries Boaz, and a marital union between Ruth and Naomi would go against the very definition of marriage implied by Gen 2:24 itself.[60] Instead, the allusion is to show that Ruth loved Naomi as her own body, joining her in covenant kinship. Indeed, Ruth's famous declaration, "[w]here you go I will go, and where

---

58. E.g., the marriages of Laban's daughters to Jacob (Gen 29); Abimelech made king (Judg 9); David made king (2 Sam 5; 1 Chr 11), David re-established as king (2 Sam 19).

59. Compare Warner, "'Therefore a Man Leaves his Father and his Mother.'"

60. See also Matt 19:3–9; Rom 1:26–27; 1 Cor 6:9.

you stay I will stay. Your people will be my people and your God my God" (Ruth 1:16–17, NIV), considering the other references to Gen 2, typifies the mantra of Gen 2:23. Readers, therefore, can infer she was an embodiment of an עזר for Naomi, loving her mother-in-law as her own bone and flesh.

Another plausible intertextual allusion to Gen 2:18–25 is in Exod 18. Moses is the lone arbiter for the people—the pronouncer of what is wise—being severely overworked. Jethro sees that it is not good that he is alone (vv. 14–18) and instructs Moses to appoint capable God-fearers to help him, so there can be peace (שלום; vv. 19–23). Then, in a redeemed echo of Gen 3:17a, Moses listens to the voice of Jethro, and the workload is successfully relieved (vv. 24–27).

Although עזר is not directly used to describe the appointed judges, the use of key Eden vocabulary and themes is striking. With it being not good that Moses determined wisdom on his own, the judges were helpers for Moses, again suggesting the problem of being alone and the concept of help are not gendered and have societal implications beyond marriage.

The New Testament also references Gen 2:18–25 in non-marital ways, especially if it is accepted that Paul's frequent use of the body metaphor—used of both marriage (Eph 5:25-33) and, as is more often, non-marriage (Rom 12:5; Eph 4:4, 12, 16, 25; 1 Cor 12:12–31)—is, in fact, an allusion to Gen 2:18–25, particularly 2:23. Indeed, Paul even appeals to being one body in relation to how to treat a neighbour in Eph 4:25 ("Therefore each of you must put off falsehood and speak truthfully to your neighbor, for we are all members of one body," NIV).

That Paul's body metaphor is rooted in Gen 2:23 can be verified from his discourse to the husbands in Eph 5. There, body imagery refers both to the body of Christ and the spousal relationship and is clearly linked to Gen 2:18–25. Not only is Gen 2:24 directly quoted in v. 31, Christ presents the church to himself, mirroring the presentation of the woman to the man in Gen 2, among other things,[61] but Christ plays the position of both

---

61. Many commentators note connection with Ezek 16:10–14. See Bock, *Ephesians*, 180; Fowl, *Ephesians*, 189–90; Lincoln, *Ephesians*, 376–77.

God and the human: the presenter and the presented to.⁶² Paul references Gen 2:22 in v. 27 and Gen 2:24 in v. 31. One would expect, therefore, a reference to Gen 2:23 in between, precisely where he calls the husbands to love their wives as their own body, as Christ does the church (vv. 28–30).⁶³

It should be emphasized that the body metaphor used here is a development of the body theme earlier (Eph 4:4–6; 1:10), but *newly* applying it to husbands and wives. As such, Paul reflects a complex understanding of Gen 2:18–25 that can see it as both foundational for marriage and foundational for the life of the Body more generally.⁶⁴ As Paul says in Rom 12:4–5, "[f]or just as each of us has one body with many members, and these members do not all have the same function, so in Christ we, though many, form one body, and each member belongs to all the others" (NIV). The church shares bone and flesh, each an עזר, and each, with their different gifts (כנגדו) for each other.

Furthermore, Jesus was single and approved it as an available life choice (Matt 19:10–12). Paul conceded that he wished everyone would stay unmarried (1 Cor 7:6–9, 32–38), and there will be no marriage in the new heavens and new earth (Mark 12:25). Indeed, when Jesus describes, and models, the ultimate expression of love—to lay down one's own bone and flesh—he does not use the example of dying for a spouse or even family, but for friends (John 15:13). Considering this, it would be shocking to find Gen 2:18–25 has such narrow applicability as to pertain to marriage alone. Indeed, if it is speaking uniquely to marriage, then the not-goodness of Gen 2:18 is not a reality for humans generally, for it could hardly be said of Jesus, Paul, or those they

---

62. Notably, God is Israel's עזר, like the woman, throughout the Old Testament.

63. Bock connects Lev 19:18, Gen 2, and Eph 5, saying, "[t]he one-flesh idea of Genesis 2:23–24 is present (Eph. 5:31) . . . In this oneness comes the unity that Paul is urging for the marriage. For a husband to love his wife is an extension of his loving and caring for himself. It also reflects the love he is to have for any person, what Scripture calls one's 'neighbour' (Lev. 19:18)" (*Ephesians*, 180). See also Wintle, *Ephesians*, 135.

64. This is consistent with Midrashic exegesis (see Pickup, "New Testament Interpretation").

taught, that it was not good for them to remain unmarried. Readers, therefore, should not be finding enduring significance in Gen 2:18. This is highly implausible given Adam's archetypal role, the connection between helping, wisdom, and morality, and the Garden's idyllic function.

As both the Old Testament and New Testament utilize Gen 2:18–25 in ways beyond marriage, the text carries broader implications. It is also unsurprising, given the theses of this paper, that the other ethical command of Jesus said to be foundational to all the Law and the Prophets is the Golden Rule, "So in everything, do to others what you would have them do to you, for this sums up the Law and the Prophets" (Matt 7:12, NIV). Notice it also appeals to oneself, just as Lev 19:18 does. Do to others like they are your very bone and flesh, one may say.

Some Implications

The scene's applicability to marriage should not be considered compromised by the view presented herein, though the assumption the text is *only* defining marriage or gender ideology must be rejected. This is dense literature designed to be meditated on day and night (Ps 1:2), fully capable of speaking to both marriage and broader relationships. Helmut Thielicke explains it well, saying, "[l]ife presents such a wealth of possibilities to love, serve, and suffer with other people that even the person who lives his life without a married partner is given the same opportunity to find and fulfil himself in devotion to others. Marriage, to which the text refers, constitutes only a kind of model for the fulfilment of love in our life."[65]

One could think of it as a foundation story for cooks. This would apply to both professional chefs and home cooks. In many respects, the two are identical—and home cooking can sometimes be better than at restaurants! There need not be two stories. However, professional chefs—who, presumably, cook also at home—have unique and formal responsibilities to certain persons. Within the story, it could be discerned what these are,

---

65. Thielicke, *How the World Began*, 91–92.

but it does not follow there would be nothing to be gleaned about home cooks.

Reading Gen 2:18–25 to include non-marital implications does, however, compromise unhelpful views of singleness. It is often difficult to side with 1 Cor 7:6–9 which says it is good to remain unmarried. In much of the world, to be single and celibate is a death sentence—to be condemned to loneliness and depression—and even a sign of shame on oneself or the community. But Jesus was single and lived the fullness of what it means to be truly human. One can hardly say it was not good for him to be single. One could say, however, that it would not have been good for him to be alone, to have lived a purely solitary life, without family, friends, or community. Jesus was indeed the second Adam, for whom it was likewise not good to be alone.

Perhaps one of the reasons a celibate life, for whatever underlying reason—one's calling, lack of mates, sexual orientation, or some other reason (Matt 19:10–12)—is considered a death sentence in Western culture is because the profound, lifegiving, covenant, עֵזֶר-friendship humans are called to be for one another has been relegated to marriage. When truly loving and relational depth—bone of bone and flesh of flesh, members of one another—can only be achieved via marriage, of course, singleness should be avoided! But if the natural human desire for intimate relationships—and this is not the same as sexual relationships—can be fulfilled outside romance, then singleness truly can be a good and fulfilling option. One may even find themselves agreeing with Paul that, though each has their gift, it is truly good to remain unmarried (1 Cor 7:6–9, 38).

There are certainly trends toward greater acceptance of singleness in some pockets of the West. Still, for an environment where neither singleness nor marriage is a default, but each a calling, both fully recognized as a worthy gift capable of relational fulfillment, it would require a momentous shift in many parts of the Western church towards a richer sense of community, alongside the elimination of singleness shaming. Will each be members of one another (Eph 4:25), bone of bone and flesh of flesh? Will each be so committed to one another in covenant friendship that no one would ever be unknown or lonely, with no love lost for singles? Could the picture of the Church in Acts 2:42–47 and 4:32–35 truly be modelled here and now?

These values must also be taught from the pulpit, which must start with Christian scholars. One of the biggest influences on how Christian leaders, pastors or otherwise, lead and shape the values of Christian communities is the scholars training, teaching, and providing resources. Though reflections and debates on marriage or gender should continue, the pertinence of the pre-sin human story to neighbours, friends, and singles deserves greater treatment from Christian scholars, which will shape pulpit teaching. Commentators should make intentional efforts to include reflections on the universally relatable significances of the text, regardless of sex or relationship status, grounding communities in the covenant friendship they are called to.

Conclusion

Leviticus 19:18 is not weighty enough to be the second great commandment. However, Gen 2:18–25, as the ideal picture of heavenly earth, would be expected to be the foundation for it and, indeed, contains several elements suggesting as much. The Tree of the Knowledge of Good and Evil, the gender-neutral problem and solution in Gen 2:18, and the covenantal, kinship body language of Gen 2:23 problematize the text as a purely marital story. Alongside non-marital allusions to the story in both the Old Testament and New Testament, it is most likely that the true root of neighbourly love is this one and only pre-sin human interaction, providing a richness to the story beyond even its depth when narrowed to marriage. Gen 2:18–25 can now consistently be seen as foundational as expected, and the obscure Lev 19:18 is no longer out of place, for it is itself not the commandment per se, but rather the best example of the commandment in propositional form within the Old Testament.

C. S. Lewis claims, "[a] man does not call a line crooked unless he has some idea of a straight line."[66] The straight line for all human relationships, modelled perfectly only by Jesus, is the

---

66. Lewis, *Mere Christianity*, 41.

second great commandment, quotable in Lev 19:18 but rooted in Gen 2:18–25. The Western church struggles to see neighbourly love in Gen 2. This is possibly because, in part, it struggles with the type of deep, lifesaving friendship humanity is called to.

Bibliography

Beale, Gregory K. "Eden, the Temple, and the Church's Mission in the New Creation." *Journal of the Evangelical Theological Society* 48 (2005) 5–31.

Bergmann, U. "עזר." In *Theological Lexicon of the Old Testament*, edited by Ernst Jenni and Claus Westermann. Translated by Mark E. Biddle, 2:872–74. Peabody, MA: Hendrickson, 1997.

Bock, Darrell. *Ephesians: An Introduction and Commentary.* Tyndale New Testament Commentaries 10. Downers Grove, IL: IVP Academic, 2019.

Buchanan, George Wesley. "The Old Testament Meaning of the Knowledge of Good and Evil." *Journal of Biblical Literature* 75 (1956) 114–20.

Clines, D. J. A. "The Image of God in Man." *Tyndale Bulletin* 19 (1968) 53–103.

———. *What Does Eve Do To Help? And Other Readerly Questions to the Old Testament.* Journal for the Study of the Old Testament Supplement Series 94. Sheffield: Sheffield Academic, 1990.

Davidson, Richard. "Earth's First Sanctuary: Genesis 1–3 and Parallel Creation Accounts." *Andrews University Seminary Studies* 53 (2015) 65–89.

Davidson, Robert. *Genesis 1–11*. Cambridge Bible Commentary. Cambridge: Cambridge University Press, 1973.

Eiselen, Frederick Carl. "The Tree of the Knowledge of Good and Evil." *The Biblical World* 36 (1910) 101–12.

Fowl, Stephen E. *Ephesians: A Commentary.* Louisville: Westminster John Knox, 2012.

France, R. T. *Matthew: An Introduction and Commentary.* Tyndale New Testament Commentaries. Downers Grove, IL: IVP Academic, 2008.

Friedman, Richard Elliott. *Commentary on the Torah.* San Francisco: HarperCollins, 2001.

Hamilton, Victor. *The Book of Genesis: Chapters 1–17.* New International Commentary on the Old Testament. Grand Rapids: Eerdmans, 1990.

Hawkins, Ralph. "Help, OT." In *The New Interpreter's Dictionary of the Bible,* edited by Katharine SakenFeld, 2:796. Nashville: Abingdon, 2007.

Hendel, Ronald. "Adam." In *Eerdmans Dictionary of the Bible,* edited by David Noel Freedman, 18–19. Grand Rapids: Eerdmans, 2000.

Hess, Richard. "Adam, Father, He: Gender Issues in Hebrew Translation." *The Bible Translator* 56 (2005) 144–53.

Hinckley, Robert. "Adam, Aaron, and the Garden Sanctuary." *Logia* 22 (2013) 5–12.

Keil, Karl F., and Franz Delitzsch, *Biblical Commentary on the Old Testament: Volume 1. The Pentateuch.* Translated by James Martin. Edinburgh: T. & T. Clark, 1869.

Kelly, Henry Ansgar. "Love of Neighbor as Great Commandment in the Time of Jesus: Grasping at Straws in the

Hebrew Scriptures." *Journal of the Evangelical Theological Society* 60 (2017) 265–81.

Koehler, Ludwig, and Walter Baumgartner. "אָדָם." In *The Hebrew and Aramaic Lexicon of the Old Testament*, edited and translated by M. E. J. Richardson, 1:14–15. New York: Brill, 1994.

———. "עֵזֶר." In *The Hebrew and Aramaic Lexicon of the Old Testament*, edited and translated by M. E. J. Richardson, 2:811–12. New York: Brill, 1995.

Lewis, C. S. *Mere Christianity*. Complete C. S. Lewis Signature Classics. New York: Harper One, 2002.

Lincoln, Andrew T. *Ephesians*. Word Biblical Commentary 42. Grand Rapids: Zondervan, 2014.

Lipiński, Louvain. "עֵזֶר." In *Theological Dictionary of the Old Testament*, edited by G. Johannes Botterweck, Helmer Ringgren, and Heinz-Josef Fabry. Translated by David E. Green, 11:12–17. Grand Rapids: Eerdmans, 2001.

Lussier, Ernest. "Adam in Genesis 1,1–4,24." *The Catholic Biblical Quarterly* 18 (1956) 137–39.

Maass, Mainz. "אָדָם." In *Theological Dictionary of the Old Testament*, edited by G. Johannes Botterweck and Helmer Ringgren. Translated by John T. Willis, 1:75–87. Grand Rapids: Eerdmans, 1977.

McKenzie, John L. *Dictionary of the Bible*. New York: Macmillan, 1965.

Middleton, J. Richard. *The Liberating Image: The Imago Dei in Genesis 1*. Grand Rapids: Brazos, 2005.

———. "Image of God." In *The Oxford Encyclopedia of the Bible and Theology*, edited by Samuel E. Bellatine, 2:516–23. Oxford: Oxford University Press, 2015.

Morales, L. Michael. *Who Shall Ascend the Mountain of the Lord? A Biblical Theology of the Book of Leviticus*. New Studies in Biblical Theology 37. Downers Grove, IL: InterVarsity, 2015.

Motyer, S. "Adam." In *New Bible Dictionary*, edited by J. D. Douglas et al., 13–15. 3rd ed. Downers Grove, IL: IVP, 1996.

Peppiatt, Lucy. *Women and Worship at Corinth: Paul's Rhetorical Arguments in 1 Corinthians*. Eugene, OR: Cascade, 2015.

Peterson, Brian Neil. *Genesis: A Pentecostal Commentary*. Pentecostal Commentary Series 8. New York: Brill, 2022.

Pickup, Martin. "New Testament Interpretation of the Old Testament: The Theological Rational for Midrashic Exegesis." *Journal of the Evangelical Theological Society* 51 (2008) 353–81.

Provan, Iain. *Discovering Genesis: Content, Interpretation, Reception*. London: SPCK, 2015.

———. *Seriously Dangerous Religion*. Waco, TX: Baylor University Press, 2014.

Rad, Gerhard von. *Genesis: A Commentary*. Translated by John H. Marks. Philadelphia: Westminster, 1956.

Renn, Stephen D., ed. *Expository Dictionary of Bible Words: Word Studies for Key English Bible Words Based on the Hebrew and Greek Texts*. Peabody, MA: Hendrickson, 2005.

Sailhamer, John. *The Pentateuch as Narrative*. Grand Rapids: Zondervan, 1992.

Sarna, Nahum. *Genesis*. Jewish Publication Society Torah Commentary. Philadelphia: Jewish Publication Society, 1989.

Steinmann, Andrew E. *Genesis*. Tyndale Old Testament Commentaries. Downers Grove, IL: IVP Academic, 2019.

Steins, David. "The Grammar of Social Gender in Biblical Hebrew." *Hebrew Studies* 49 (2008) 7–26.

Taylor, Marion Ann, and Heather E. Weir. *Let Her Speak for Herself: Nineteenth-Century Women Writing on Women in Genesis*. Waco, TX: Baylor University Press, 2006.

Thielicke, Helmut. *How the World Began: Man in the First Chapters of the Bible*. Translated by John W. Doberstein. Philadelphia: Muhlenberg, 1960.

Tosato, Angelo. "On Genesis 2:24." *The Catholic Biblical Quarterly* 52 (1990) 389–409.

Turner-Smith, Sarah. "Naked But Not Ashamed: A Reading of Genesis 2:25 in Textual and Cultural Context." *The Journal of Theological Studies* 69 (2018) 425–46.

Wallace, Howard. "Adam." In *The Anchor Bible Dictionary*, edited by David Noel Freedman, 1:62–64. New York: Doubleday, 1992.

———. "Tree of Knowledge and Tree of Life." In *The Anchor Bible Dictionary*, edited by David Noel Freedman, 6:656–60. New York: Doubleday, 1992.

Waltke, Bruce. *Genesis: A Commentary*. Grand Rapids: Zondervan, 2001.

Walton, John H. *The Lost World of Adam and Eve.* Downers Grove, IL: IVP Academic, 2015.

———. *Genesis.* The NIV Application Commentary. Grand Rapids: Zondervan, 2001.

Warner, Megan. "'Therefore a Man Leaves his Father and his Mother and Clings to his Wife': Marriage and Intermarriage in Genesis 2:24." *Journal of Biblical Literature* 136 (2017) 269–88.

Wenham, Gordon. *Genesis 1–15.* Word Biblical Commentary. Grand Rapids: Zondervan, 2014 [1987].

Westermann, Claus. "אָדָם." In *Theological Lexicon of the Old Testament*, edited by Ernst Jenni and Claus Westermann. Translated by Mark E. Biddle, 1:31–42. Peabody, MA: Hendrickson, 1997.

Wintle, Brian. *Ephesians: A Pastoral and Contextual Commentary.* Asia Bible Commentary Series. Carlisle: Langham, 2020.

SUNRISE AND MOONSET:
THE LORD BEHIND AND BEFORE

Susan Cowger[1]
Cheney, WA, USA

Like out in the wilds
enduring a whole year of camping
out in the wilds   she's brrr-cold despite the best
down bag   Every morn squirming into jeans
sweatshirt & socks   hating to leave
that tent   the warm sack   breakfast sizzling

over tinder and sparks   That is until one day
a new dawn shrugs
says *Time* to go
And no   no fire this morning

No more fire
She's told   *Stand in the light*
So that's what she does   Stands   Faces the sun

Her beloved turns the other way
Keeping an eye on dubious shadows
he readies for the unknown   facing
the depth of darkness   edging his whole being
into the uncharted
hoping to God   he has her back
Hoping like hell   God has his

---

1. Susan Cowger's third book, *Hawk & Songbird* (Cascade), will be released in 2024. Others include *Slender Warble* (Cascade [2020]) and a chapbook *Scarab Hiding* (Finishing Line [2006]). Poems have appeared in many journals and anthologies.

COYOTE ALIVE

I saw coyote again   loping
through the brume   as if
unwavering wind was on his side   That is
until he saw the walkers of dawn
and had to choose

between man afoot
and the narrow path between houses
One day I suppose someone
will trap or shoot him   all bravado
and pride   Who in the world
wants wild hope   stuffed & dusty
hunkered down in the den   But there I am

at the window every morning
scanning dawn
for untamed movement   a nod of wind
feral fear giving hope
another chance to be lithe

TRANSFIGURATION

I wonder if he arrives early
and sees the children
scatter and scour the bookshelves and floor
Under beds   behind the piano   the littles
whisper to each other   *Where is it?*
Where IS it?   The book   That one   you know the one
One sofa   two cushions   too crowded
for everyone to have a good seat   I wonder
if he is surprised how long his stories hold the children
gazing straight ahead   Imagine
coaxing them into a furious climb   joining
the unflinching scale   casting off rope & axe

As a last resort   suspending all disbelief
Somewhere near the top

ahead of them   he stops

their mouths open
As if this is the final switchback
every child turns from the pages to look at his face
watch

and there it is   How long did it take
to hear again his baritone
from the edge of the world

Do not be afraid

Wisdom of Speech:
Book of Analects and Book of James

Chiaen Liu
China Evangelical Graduate School of Theology, Taoyuan City, Taiwan

Introduction

Speech plays a vital role in our daily activities. There are two ancient Chinese statements: "One who knows does not talk; one who talks does not know"; and "Speak when it is time to speak."[1] The timing of speaking stands as the central key in Chinese culture. The Scriptures also indicate the importance of one's speech. In some of the Wisdom books, especially the Old Testament and Old Testament Pseudepigrapha, there are also many teachings about speech, such as "a man of understanding remains silent" (Prov 11:12, ESV); "before you speak, learn" (Sir 18:19); or "others keep silent because they know when to speak" (Sir 20:6). From these statements, one can see that the manner and timing of speaking are crucially important for all people regardless of their cultures. Speech can either encourage or destroy people. A word spoken incorrectly can impede communication, but a word aptly uttered can lead to understanding.[2] Different cultures have developed their philosophical concepts of speaking.

Since the book of *Analects* and the Bible are two important books in the Eastern and Western cultures, this paper starts from analyzing these two books to understand the different concepts of speech. The book of *Analects* which preserves lectures of the great Chinese master Confucius will be a helpful starting point to

---

1. Lao-Tzu, *Teachings*, 56; Confucius, *Analects*, 14:13.
2. English, *Theology Remixed*, 106.

understand Chinese wisdom in terms of the manner of speech.[3] Unfortunately, there is no consensus among scholars about the issue of how to read the *Analects*. Some people propose that one should focus on semantics, syntax, and pragmatics to understand this book. On the other hand, other people point out that one should pay more attention to the rationale in order to really catch the deeper ideas. There are many pieces of unknown information in each chapter of the *Analects* (names, or reasons for the sayings).[4] The book of *Analects* is not a systematic work but an act of collective memory.[5] Therefore, these pieces of memory will provide good resources for readers to tease out the concept of speech in the Chinese culture through Confucius's works, especially his speeches and dialogues with his students. This paper will attempt to focus on the ideas and rationales through the Chinese culture and Confucius framework to understand the ethical concerns of speech.

In Scripture, speech is usually related to the understanding of wisdom (Jas 1:19; Sir 5:11; Eccl 5:1). Wisdom is usually regarded as a measure of human behavior, including speaking, and this pattern can also be found in Proverbs (1:7; 2:6; 22:4), Sirach (1:1, 14, 26; 19:20), and Wisdom of Solomon (1:6; 7:15).[6] In this case, while one wants to tease out ideas of speech from the New Testament, it is inevitable to analyze the book of James, especially 3:1—4:10.[7] Since the passage of Jas 3:1—4:10 is regarded as Scripture, one can employ a proper method to understand the manner of speech through analyzing the language. Comparing Chinese culture and the teachings in the Bible will provide a framework for discerning the teachings about effective speaking. This paper will demonstrate distinct rationales lead to various understandings of speeches in the *Analects* of Confucius and in the Bible. Therefore, one can see the different theological

3. Confucius is called the model teacher of every age in Chinese culture.
4. Qian, *Kong Zi*, 5–13.
5. *The Analects* was not written by a single author but written on bamboo strips by the disciples of Confucius (see Martin, "Understanding the Confucian Analects," 75).
6. Varner, *Book of James*, 29–30.
7. Varner, *Book of James*, 116.

foundations of these two works, focusing on the role of God in one's daily life. In this case, this paper argues that the order of creation and limits between creatures that God set serve as the critical point for understanding ethical issues in speaking. In other words, the creature was made in order, and following this order establishes boundaries between different living beings. But in the model of Confucius, the discussion focuses on the horizontal relationship among people, without the vertical concept of God. This model is the significant difference between Confucian and Christian thoughts, and therefore, a Christian who has been influenced by Confucian ideas needs to be aware of this issue and establish a more robust theology, not just focusing on social relationships.

Methodology and Theory

Ancient Chinese Culture and Confucius

The book of *Analects* is a scattered collection of speeches, and the method of studying this book should start from the Chinese cultural background, especially the understanding of Confucius's thoughts. In ancient China, human beings were the focus of attention. There is an old saying, "[m]an [and woman] excels all the beings in heaven and on earth." The ancient Chinese regarded societal structure to be more important than the benefits to individual beings, and it has served as a distinct foundation of moral order.[8] Chinese people took the natural distinctions of age, sex, and family relationships very seriously because they thought these were a part of nature.[9] The law which was revealed in nature was an essential factor that enabled people to determine how to act.[10]

The Chinese concept of "heaven," however, simply refers to the laws of nature. People observe nature and synthesize general

---

8. H. F. Rudd, *Chinese Moral Sentiments before Confucius: A Study in the Origin of Ethical Valuations* (Shanghai: Christian Literature Society Depot, 1915), 88.
9. Rudd, *Chinese Moral Sentiments*, 116.
10. Taylor, *Sources*, 87.

principles, especially the relationships among human beings. Therefore, social order is the focus, and family life becomes the major area in which people establish their personalities.[11] Within the family, distinctions are identified by age, experience, wisdom, etc. Senior members provide protection of and affection for the young whereas the younger generation is characterized by immaturity, dependence, and obedience.[12] There are five types of relationships which Chinese people are concerned with: ruler and subject; parent and child; husband and wife; elder and younger brother; and between friends. Three of them are practiced in the family and the other two in society.[13] The family system established the foundation of society and was the place for human beings to practice morality. Almost all philosophers develop their ideas using this scheme. There was a period in which different schools of thought debated thousands of years ago. It is known as the period of the Spring and Autumn and the Warring States (770–221 BCE). Among all philosophers at this time, one of them was the most well-known Confucius (551–479 BCE), who influenced China's history, politics, and thoughts for more than two thousand years.

The Foundation of Confucius's Ethics

Confucius's central idea is that human beings should cherish the aspiration to become superior to who they were in their past and who they are in the present.[14] In Confucius's mind, *li* (禮; "forms of social intercourse") and *jen* (仁; "benevolence") are basic principles of social discipline.[15] For him, *li* is the principle which the ancient kings established. It combined the laws of heaven and regulated the expressions of human nature.

---

11. Rudd, *Chinese Moral Sentiments*, 72–73.
12. Rudd, *Chinese Moral Sentiments*, 117.
13. Rudd, *Chinese Moral Sentiments*, 134.
14. Dawson, *Ethics*, 1.
15. There is the third category *yi* (義; "righteousness"). This concept, however, refers to social justice, which provides the most appropriate way to make a profit. Therefore, the analysis can merge *yi* into the discussion of *li* since they both talk about the maintenance of social order among people (see Confucius, *Wisdom*, 157).

Therefore, the one who has attained *li* lives; the one who has lost it dies:

> This *li* is based on the form set up in the heaven and patterned on the earth. *li* deals with the worship of the spirits and is extended to the rites and ceremonies of funerals, sacrifices to ancestors, archery, carriage driving, "capping," marriage, and court audience or exchange of diplomatic visits.[16]

The good things are confidence and peace; the bad things are struggle, robbery, and murder. *Jen* is the root of humanity and serves as the highest moral standard. To subdue oneself and return to propriety is *jen*.[17] The social orders between prince and minister or father and son were Confucius's central concerns, and he believed that the social relationship is definitely the place to manifest *jen*.[18] As for the relationship of these three, Confucius proclaimed the concept of *tao* (道; "path"). *Tao* was understood as the focus of ethics in ancient China, which could be characterized as *li* and *jen*. Confucius's *tao* talks about the principles of maintaining proper social order which can be attained through education.[19] It is more concerned with natural law and how planets operate. This does not mean that Confucius did not care about natural laws, but he used a different way, tracing these laws by observing the relationships among people. Confucius was deeply attracted by pursuing *tao*. He said, "[i]f a person in the morning hears the right path (*tao*), he may die in the evening without regret."[20] In terms of Confucius's *tao*, he took *jen* as the way to connect all his concepts and there are two components of *jen*: *chung* and *shu*. *Chung* refers to the will to help others and do one's best, and *shu* is not to give others what we do not like and being consistent to oneself.[21] Based on the understanding, people who have *jen* will speak faithfully to be

---

16. Confucius, *Wisdom*, 158.
17. Confucius, *Analects*, 12:1.
18. Song, *Zhong Yong Jin Zhu Jin Yi*, 1.
19. Qian, *Kong Zi*, 97–105.
20. Confucius, *Analects*, 4:8.
21. Confucius, *Analects*, 15:24.

the best of themselves and consist in themselves.[22] He says, "[m]y doctrine is that of an all-pervading unity," and his student Zeng says, "[t]he doctrine of our master is to be true to the principles of our nature (*chung*) and the benevolent exercise of them to others (*shu*). This [the doctrine of our master] is nothing more [than these two]."[23] In addition, Confucius asserted the concept of *kuan* ("pass-through"), which means "a thread for stringing holed, copper coins through a hole."[24] The ideas of *chung* and *shu* are highly associated with social relationships from both the positive and negative sides. They serve as manners of representing the central idea of *kuan*. Confucius started from the relationships among people to discuss the concept of *tao-kuan* (passing through the path), but had nothing to do with gods, although he did not deny their existence. In practice, Confucius clearly distinguished two kinds of people: *junzi* (君子; "best moral self") and *xiaojen* (小人; "immature moral self"), with the criteria of practicing *li*, *jen*, or not. He paid attention to the *tao* of *junzi* (君子之道), which is based on filial piety. And the three aspects of practicing this *tao* are: relationship; reign; and destiny.[25] The concept of reign is also a type of relationship among people whereas destiny is related to the relationship between human beings and heaven.[26] Relationship exposes the concepts of these two and becomes the most significant element to understand Confucius's philosophy which is centered on human beings and their relationship.[27]

A Linguistic Model
Since people take the book of James as Scripture, a more text-based methodology will be a better way to analyze the text. In this case, Halliday's Systemic Functional Linguistics (SFL) will

22. Frisina, "Ritual."
23. Confucius, *Analects*, 4:15.
24. Cua, "Possibility."
25. Chen, *Kong Xue Lun Ji*, 223–35.
26. The concept of heaven in Chinese culture is an abstract idea. It is not a "person" but refers to a principle which has been practiced in the cosmos for a long time.
27. Qian, *Kong Zi*, 210.

be a helpful tool since it focuses on trusting the text.[28] There are many topics or themes in this book, and the passage Jas 3:1—4:10 is the prominent section to describe this issue. To control one's tongue is a clear teaching in this passage, but this passage would be easily regarded as a moral exhortation. In addition, this passage can help us to understand the relationship between God and this moral teaching. Employing a proper method of interpretation will help us gain a better understanding. According to Brown and Yule, "topic is clearly an intuitively satisfactory way of describing the unifying principle which makes one stretch of discourse 'about' something and the next stretch of discourse 'about' something else."[29] Hence, this paper will employ a discourse analysis approach in order to help arrive at a meaning within this passage which will give us more understandings about speeches. Discourse-analysis approaches involve various categories, and one of them is *cohesion*. Martin Dibelius points out that in the book of James, "there is not only a lack of continuity in thought between individual sayings and other smaller units, but also between larger treaties."[30] Nevertheless, one can still find cohesion while employing a proper linguistic approach to this book.[31] In this case, the book of James consists of "a text with high cohesion, high cohesive interaction, and hence high cohesive harmony."[32] Since "texts cohere or hold together in a unified way,"[33] *cohesion* serves as an important factor to discern what the topic is.[34] The biblical texts usually provide elements that creates cohesion with patterns of continuity.[35] In order to trace the cohesion in a passage, we may employ the ideas of semantic and participant chains and with the analysis of the interaction of these elements, we can recognize the central concept

---

28. Westfall, "Mapping the Text," 13.
29. Brown and Yule, *Discourse Analysis*, 75.
30. Dibelius, *James*, 2.
31. Porter, "Cohesion."
32. Porter, "Cohesion," 67.
33. Porter, *Idioms*, 304.
34. Givón, *On Understanding Grammar*, 298–99.
35. Westfall, "Mapping the Text," 14.

of the topic by tracing the information flow.[36] The words which are in the same semantic domain may establish various chains. Participant chains, on the other hand, refer to the repetition of the characters which are indicated by nouns, verbs, or pronouns.[37]

The last criterion for determining the topic of discourse is the relationship to the co-text (literary context). Brown and Yule state, "[t]ext creates its own context."[38] Misinterpretations may result from neglecting the co-text.[39] Lexical, semantic, and grammatical elements serve as important factors for us to understand the relationship to the co-text.[40] Therefore, the steps of analysis will include the following: (1) identifying the semantic and participant chains; (2) probing the relationship of the chains; (3) and recognizing the relationship to the co-text.[41]

Analects' Model on Speech—Confucius's Ethics on Speech

Since *li* and *jen* are central ideas in the system of Confucius, one should tease out his ethics on the speech from these perspectives. Propriety is the most important rule to explain the right relationships with others, and the chief one is revealed under the manner of *li*.[42]

Li (禮) from the Model of Junzi (君子)

One's speech should follow the natural sequence, which is called *li*.[43] The heaven does not speak, but the four seasons run their course, and therefore, human beings would much rather not talk.[44] In this case, although natural laws should serve as the

---

36. The interaction between semantics and participant chains will serve as a means to find the topic of a passage (i.e., what the text is talking about). More details can be found in Liu, "What a Story Is about."
37. Westfall, "Blessed Be the Ties."
38. Brown and Yule, *Discourse Analysis*, 50.
39. Gorman, *Elements*, 69–71.
40. Westfall, "Mapping the Text," 17.
41. Westfall, *Discourse Analysis*, 28–87.
42. Dawson, *Ethics*, 98.
43. Defoort, "Confucius."
44. Confucius, *Analects* (Waley), 235.

standard for people to trace the order. People will recognize the rationale by observing the changes of the seasons and the life or death of grain, but it does not provide enough information for people to learn how to speak.[45] One needs to turn to pay attention to the relationship between human beings in order to understand the idea of *li* and to probe into the ethics of using speech.

In addition, in Confucius's framework, *jen* (仁; "benevolence") is a serious issue which is explained according to the understanding of human beings and their actions.[46] *Junzi*, which Confucius asserted as a perfect model for *li*, is a virtuous person who perfectly controls the idea of wisdom, and focuses on practical issues, especially those of the family and public administration, and seeks to solve ethical and political problems.[47]

Confucius depicted an image of the virtuous person concerning the idea of speech. He proposed that a *junzi* should act without violence and speak without vulgarity.[48] The superior person is quick in action but cautious in speech, is free from worries and fears, and is ashamed of his word outstripping his deed.[49] Confucius says, "[l]ook not at what is contrary to propriety; listen not to what is contrary to propriety; speak not about what is contrary to propriety; make no movement which is contrary to propriety."[50] One will know what to do and when to do it when this person knows the proper boundary between people, which is the real function of *li*, and it will show the real *jen*.[51] This person may not know everything; however, he or she does not widely comment on things he or she does not understand, but when this person names something, the name is sure to be usable in speech, and when this person says something, that is sure to be

---

45. Wong, *Ju Chia Ti Chung Ho Kuan*, 96–98.
46. Qian, *Kong Zi*, 47–48.
47. Yao, *Wisdom*, 214.
48. Yao, *Wisdom*, 143.
49. Confucius, *Analects*, 14:27.
50. Confucius, *Analects*, 12:1.
51. Nan, *Lun Yu*, 53.

practicable.[52] This person seldom speaks; when he or she does, it is sure that he or she will be right on the mark.[53]

Wisdom of Society and the Manner of Modesty

The wisdom of society and the manner of modesty are the foundations of speaking. Wise people should also be humble and have a keen sense of observing the social order. According to Confucius, "he [or she] who speaks without modesty will find it hard to make his [or her] words good."[54] Furthermore, words also serve as a touchstone to knowing people. In particular, a person can be regarded as wise or foolish by speech. It is said, "[w]ithout knowing the force of words, it is impossible to know people."[55] "For one word a person is often deemed to be wise and for one word he [or she] is often deemed to be foolish."[56] In Confucius's idea, there is a significant difference between "wise" and "clever." The wise are virtuous, although they are slow to speak.[57] The clever are immoral, although they seem always to manage "clever talking."[58] Confucius held a high suspicion about those who talk nicely. He said, "clever talk and pretentious manner are seldom found in the good."[59] One will become wise through education and learning from the social relationship.[60]

Therefore, the pursuit of wisdom is centered on a way of stabilization, being disciplined, and being shaped in the changeable stream of human experiences, and in the Confucian tradition is to establish a framework of formal roles, relationships, and institutions.[61] Confucian concepts of wisdom are connected with moral practices, not only abstract ideas. Since society and human

---

52. Confucius, *Analects*, 13:3.
53. Confucius, *Analects*, 11:14.
54. Confucius, *Analects*, 14:20.
55. Confucius, *Analects*, 20:3.
56. Confucius, *Analects*, 19:25.
57. Confucius, *Analects*, 13:27.
58. Confucius, *Analects*, 1:3.
59. Confucius, *Analects*, 1:3.
60. Yang, *Kong Xue Si Lun*, 51.
61. Ames, "Thinking," 103–4.

ethics are the main concerns of Confucianism, Chinese intellectuals usually seek unification between learning and action by practicing social responsibility with morality and knowledge.[62] In Confucius's expression, wisdom has its outward appearance, which is woven into *jen*.[63] The wisdom of how to respond and when to advance or retreat, is the condition for being a *junzi*. Besides, Chinese culture developed a philosophy of instinct. Farmers who work on the ground will become *jen-zhe* (仁者; "people of benevolence") who appreciate mountains while merchants who travel along the seashore will become *zhi-zhe* (知者; "sages") who love bodies of water. In his system, Confucius adopts naturalism to depict heaven as the law of nature which does not speak and employs humanism to put human beings in the center of culture.[64] The harmony between the cosmological order and human order opens a path to distinguish good from evil, right from wrong, proper from improper.[65]

Biblical Model of Speech—Analysis of James 3

Now we will focus on the teachings from the Scripture about speech. There are many teachings about speech in the Hebrew Bible, especially in Proverbs (e.g., 10:8, 11, 21; 11:9; 12:18, 25; 13:3; 16:27; 17:14; 18:7, 21; 26:22, etc.). Sages have noted that speaking well was very important in ancient Israel. The manner of talking continues to develop in the New Testament. In the epistle of James, the author holds in high value using one's tongue. James says, "[i]f anyone is never at fault in what he says, he is a perfect man (Jas 3:2, NIV)." Therefore, it is worth analyzing this passage to obtain a clearer image of the way to talk and understand the principles of speech in the Bible. In the following section, we will focus on this passage in James to discuss the idea of controlling tongues in the Bible.

---

62. Junren, "Reasons," 94.
63. Yao, *Wisdom*, 210.
64. Jiang, "Kongzi," 50.
65. Bo, "Debate," 558; Yao, *Wisdom*, 16–17.

Identify the Discourse

Before we analyze the text further, we have to identify the discourse.[66] The phrase ἀδελφοί μου ("my brothers [and sisters]") is followed by the imperative γίνεσθε ("become") in 3:1, following the perfect participle εἰδότες ("know") and serving as a solid marker to divide units from others. Prominence occurs along with a shift from the second-person plural to the first-person plural form. And this shift is followed by the causal clause (πολλὰ γὰρ πταίομεν ἅπαντες, "for all of us make many mistakes") which remains the use of the first-person plural form.[67] This combination (the use of ἀδελφοί with an imperative) also appears in 4:11, creating another boundary marker. One can notice that the phrase ἀδελφοί μου is also used in 3:10 and 3:12. Since in both these two cases, however, this phrase is not connected with an imperative, they stand for other signs to group sub-units, rather than the macro-units.[68] Furthermore, the particle ἰδού ("behold") is used twice in 3:4 and 3:5. The use of this particle and the change of person and number from the form of the first plural to the form of the third singular in 3:4 mark sub-units of 3:4–5a and 3:5b–10a. The verb γεγονότας ("become") with the perfect tense in 3:9 draws the attention of readers to emphasize the importance of taming the tongue as subduing the creature not to curse those who have been made in the likeness of God.[69] In addition, the repetitions of σοφός ("wise") and εἰρήνη ("peace") in vv. 13–18 form cohesive ties that link these verses together.[70] In 3:13, the use of interrogative τίς ("who") indicates the idea of wisdom, which leads the discussion in the

---

66. Cheung and Bauckham, *Genre*, 75.
67. Westfall, "Analysis"; Reed, *Discourse Analysis*, 105–6.
68. Cheung and Bauckham, *Genre*, 65.
69. Hartin and Harrington, *James*, 179.
70. According to Stoddard (*Text and Texture: Patterns of Cohesion*, 15), "[c]ohesion occurs 'where the interpretation of some element in the discourse is dependent on another,' because one presupposes the other so that each pair of dependent/independent elements creates a 'cohesive tie.'". Furthermore, Martin asserts that the use of the word σοφίας at 3:13 and 3:17 establish an *inclusio*. But the repetition of the word εἰρήνην at 1:17 and 1:18 seems to glue these two verses together (Martin, *James*, 125).

following verses to distinguish the wisdom above from earthly wisdom.[71] This repeated usage of σοφία ("wisdom") in 3:13, 3:15, and 3:17 not only groups a sub-unit but also provides a clue of the relationship between wisdom and life conduct. In Jas 4, the adverb πόθεν ("whence") provides a new starting point for the discussion. However, it is still associated with the previous topic.[72] Along with the question of "do you not know" in 4:4, the vocative noun μοιχαλίδες ("adulteresses") produces a new point to start a new sub-set. Similarly, the vocative usage in 4:8 also provides another beginning.[73] The contrast between the terms of εἰρήνην (3:18) and πόλεμοι ("war," 4:1) glues the passages 3:13–18 and 4:1–10 together. Further, the author uses the second person plural pronoun "you" from 3:13 to 4:10. In this case, the passage 3:13–18 can serve as a transition for 3:1–12 and 4:1–10.[74] Therefore, the passage Jas 3:1—4:10 should be regarded as a completed section for the analysis.

Semantic and Participant Chains

Apart from the repetition of the same lexical items, the theory of Louw and Nida provides a helpful tool to trace the words within the same semantic domain which form semantic chains.[75] In 3:1–10a, there are several semantic chains worth noticing. The first is the chain of Moral and Ethical Qualities and Related Behavior (Louw and Nida's Semantic Domain 88), which occurs five

71. The term σοφός ("wise") is pointed out at the beginning of the question, which indicates that the topic of this passage is wisdom (see Varner, *Book of James*, 373).

72. Moo, *James*, 167.

73. The pattern in 4:8 (imperative + accusative + vocative) sets up a parallel.

74. Cheung and Bauckham, *Genre*, 76–77.

75. The categories of semantic domains can be seen in Louw and Nida, *Greek–English Lexicon* (note that I refer to their work as LN in this paper). Westfall writes, "[s]emantic chains are formed by lexis that share the same semantic domains. Participant ties and chains are formed by noun phrases, pronouns and verbs that refer to the same person . . . When two words that share a semantic domain occur in the same context, their meaning is constrained" ("Blessed Be the Ties," 11).

times.⁷⁶ The next chain is in the domain of Body, Body Parts, and Body Products (Domain 8), which occurs eleven times.⁷⁷ These words which are related to the physical body establish a clear cohesive tie.⁷⁸ The third one is the domain of Communication (Domain 33), which occurs seven times.⁷⁹ In 3:10b–11, the contrast between "sweet" and "bitter" serves to set up a cohesive tie of the domain of Features of Objects (Domain 79).⁸⁰ There is an essential chain of Domain 88 in 3:12–18, which occurs fourteen times.⁸¹ From the repetitions of εἰρήνη in 3:17 and v.18 and ποιέω ("do") in 3:12 and 3:18 establish other two cohesive ties. Besides, we can observe another significant chain that runs throughout the whole chapter and refers to the domain of Be, Become, Exist, and Happen (Domain 13).⁸² The discussion of morality persists in 4:1–10 and the words in this domain are used ten times to carry on the chain of morality.⁸³ The semantic chain

---

76. The words are πταίομεν (LN 88.291), πταίει (LN 88.291) and χαλιναγωγῆσαι (LN 88.85) in 3:2, ἀδικίας (LN 88.21) in 3:6, and κακόν (LN 88.106) in 3:8.
77. These are στόματα (LN 8.19) and σῶμα (LN 8.1) in 3:3, γλῶσσα (LN 8.21) and μέλος (LN 8.9) in 3:5, γλῶσσα (LN 8.21), γλῶσσα (LN 8.21), μέλεσιν (LN 8.9), and σῶμα (LN 8.1) in 3:6, γλῶσσαν (LN 8.21), ἰοῦ (LN 8.74) in 3:8, and στόματος (LN 8.19) in 3:10a.
78. Cheung and Bauckham, *Genre*, 75.
79. The words which are in the same domain are διδάσκαλοι (LN 33.243) in 3:1, λόγῳ (LN 33.99) in 3:2, πείθεσθαι (LN 33.301) in 3:3, αὐχεῖ (LN 33.368) in 3:5, εὐλογοῦμεν (LN 33.356) and καταρώμεθα (LN 33.471) in 3:9, and εὐλογία (LN 33.356) in 3:10.
80. γλυκύ (LN 79.39) and πικρόν (LN 79.41).
81. These are καλῆς (LN 88.4) and πραΰτητι (88.59) in 3:13, ζῆλον (LN 88.162), ἐριθείαν (LN 88.167), and κατακαυχᾶσθε (LN 88.194) in 3:14, ζῆλος (LN 88.162), ἐριθεία (LN 88.167), and φαῦλον (LN 88.116) in 3:16, ἁγνή (LN 88.28), ἐπιεικής (LN 88.63), ἐλέους (LN 88.76), ἀγαθῶν (LN 88.1), and ἀδιάκριτος (LN 88.242) in 3:17, and δικαιοσύνης (LN 88.13) in 3:18.
82. The words are γίνεσθε (LN 13.48) in 3:1, ὄντα (LN 13.1) in 3:4, ἐστίν (LN 13.1) in 3:5, καθίσταται (LN 13.9) and γενέσεως (LN 13.71) in 3:6, γεγονότας (LN 13.48) in 3:9, γίνεσθαι (LN 13.48) in 3:10, ποιῆσαι (LN 13.9) twice in 3:12, ἔστιν (LN 13.1) in 3:15, ἔστιν (LN 13.1) in 3:17, ποιοῦσιν (LN 13.9) in 3:18, καθίσταται (LN 13.9) in 4:4.
83. The words are κακῶς (LN 88.106) in 3:3, μοιχαλίδες (LN 88.278) in 3:4, φθόνον (LN 88.160) in 3:5, χάριν (LN 88.66; twice in this verse),

of Domain 33 also continues in this passage, with the cognitive words (αἰτεῖσθαι ["ask"], γραφή [Scripture], and λέγει ["say"]). This concept is a little different in 4:1–10 from that in the previous chapter for the communication has shifted from humans to God.[84] Before analyzing how these chains are used in this passage, one needs to pay attention to participant chains as well.

After determining the semantic chains, we now come to identify participants. In this passage, the first participant chain refers to the believers. In 3:1, the author encourages the recipients that many should not become teachers. Therefore, the cohesive tie is linked by the chain from πολλοί ("many") through διδάσκαλοι ("teachers") and the verb γίνεσθε ("be") to the phrase ἀδελφοί μου. After that, the readers also serve as the subject of εἰδότες ("know") and λημψόμεθα ("receive") in 3:1, the subject of πταίομεν ("stumble") in 3:2, and the actor of βάλλομεν ("put") in 3:3. Then in 3:6, the author indicates the pronoun ἡμῶν ("us") and continues to center the discussion around "us" being the subject of the verbs εὐλογοῦμεν ("bless") and καταρώμεθα ("curse") in 3:9. The phrase ἀδελφοί μου occurs again in 3:10 and 3:12. In 3:13–14, the author changes to the second person plural pronoun as a signal to the recipients that the second person plural pronoun becomes the subject of the verbs ἔχετε ("have"), κατακαυχᾶσθε ("boast"), and ψεύδεσθε ("lie") in 3:14. In 4:1–10, the discussion remains focusing on this participant, which is about the believers. The pronoun "you" occurs several times, and the second person plural form is used for the verbs throughout the whole passage. Furthermore, the first-person plural form is frequently used in this passage (3:1–3, 9). This usage establishes a participant chain to represent the editorial "we" and to reflect the idea of self-designation. In other words, the author switches between the first person plural and the second person plural to draw at-

---

ὑπερηφάνοις (LN 88.214), and ταπεινοῖς (LN 88.52) in 3:6, ἁμαρτωλοί (LN 88.295) and ἁγνίσατε (LN 88.30) in 3:8, and ταπεινώθητε (LN 88.56) in 3:10.

84. The word αἰτεῖσθαι (LN 33.163) which is used in 4:2 and 4:3 refers to words to God, whereas the other two words γραφή (LN 33.53) in 4:5 and λέγει (LN 33.69) in 4:5 and 4:6 are talking about the words from God.

tention from the recipients that they should learn lessons from the author.[85]

Besides, there is a separation among the community of believers. It seems that this group is divided into two categories which can be recognized within this contrast. The discrepancy indicates two different kinds of life, characteristics, and virtues. The first part refers to those who make no mistakes in speaking, are perfect (3:2), show that their works are done with gentleness born of wisdom by their good lives (3:13), have wisdom from above which is peaceable, gentle, willing to yield, full of mercy and good fruit, without a trace of partiality or hypocrisy (3:17), and a harvest of righteousness which is sown in peace (3:18). The second group refers to those who are opposite, who cannot control the tongue, boasting of great exploits (3:5), praising God and cursing people with the same mouth (3:9–10); they have bitter envy and selfish ambition in their hearts (3:14) and are earthly, unspiritual, and devilish (3:15). The author indicates that "we" all stumble, and the conditional statement with εἴ ("if") represents a hypothetical situation.[86] These two kinds of people become a contrast which continues in 4:1–10, talking about those who do whatever they want which causes fight and killing on the one hand. On the other hand, the ones who submit themselves to God and receive God's grace with humility are mentioned in this passage.

Another important participant in this passage is God, who is indicated as the Lord and Father in 3:9 and serves as the object of εὐλογία ("blessing") in 3:10. After that, the adverb ἄνωθεν ("from above") is used twice in 3:15 and 3:17, which also refers to God as the origin. In addition, the author points out this participant in 4:4 to contrast the world and God, with a quotation in 4:5 and 4:6. Then God becomes the key figure for the author to encourage the readers to cleanse themselves and resist the devil.

There is another chain that needs to be noticed. In v.3, ἵππων ("horse," LN 4.29) is mentioned and in v. 7, θηρίων ("wild beast," LN 4.3), πετεινῶν ("bird," LN 4.38), ἑρπετῶν ("reptile,"

---

85. Varner, *James*, 326.
86. Varner, *James*, 329.

LN 4.51), and ἐναλίων ("things in the sea," LN 4.58) are used. These words refer to different kinds of animals. On the other hand, συκῆ ("fig tree," LN 3.5), ἐλαίας ("olive tree," LN 3.9), ἄμπελος ("vine," LN 3.27), and σῦκα ("fig," LN 3.5) are indicated in v. 12 which are in the domain of plants. In addition, natural substances are also pointed out in this passage, such as πῦρ ("fire," LN 2.3) in 3:5 and 3:6, ὕδωρ ("water," LN 2.7) in 3:12. All these refer to the creature of God.

Interaction between Semantic and Participant Chains
In this passage, there are four semantic chains and three participant chains threading through the whole passage. The author uses the concept of part and whole to emphasize the effects of the tongue. Frequently the image of a body is described to indicate that although the tongue is a small member, it can cause a huge disaster. This expression indicates that the chain of Domain 8 is associated with Domain 33, and therefore, the body part that the author focuses on is the tongue. From the interaction between these two, the importance of learning how to speak is emphasized.[87] Furthermore, the concepts of morality and speech are related in this passage. The author points out that those who make no mistakes in speaking are perfect. Accordingly, the tongue can be an evil creature, which is full of deadly poison. The results of misusing tongue occur in 3:13–18, where the author continues discussing how the tongues would influence the "entire body (3:6)."[88] The contrast between the wisdom from above and the earthly wisdom develops in 4:1–10, and serves as the outcomes of the wisdom not from above.[89] People who have the wisdom from above will not boast about one's ambition nor deny the truth, whereas earthly wisdom will cause disorder and wickedness. One of these moral acts of behavior is the way people talk. Similarly, words within the semantic domain of being become an explicit instruction of telling the differences between order and

---

87. Tongue is usually used as a symbol of speech (see Louw and Nida, *Greek–English Lexicon*, 97).
88. Martin, *James*, 127.
89. Martin, *James*, 142.

disorder. Wisdom from above or below also serves as a criterion to describe the contrast in this passage. Therefore, the topic in this passage is that morality is highly related to wisdom, and speech is the means of distinguishing the heavenly wisdom from earthly wisdom. God plays the central role, giving true wisdom for people to control their tongues well; communication with God becomes the foundation of communicating well with people. God's creation also plays an important role in this passage. It seems that the creature of God represents the natural order, which manifests the wisdom of the work of creation. God is the one who creates all creatures and is the one who gives wisdom from above. This connects the relationship of God, wisdom, creation, speech, and moral conduct.

Relationship to the Co-Text
Many scholars take Jas 3 as a new passage that links to the topic of speech in 1:19–21.[90] This passage, however, is also related to 1:26 where the teaching of wisdom is discussed. The topic of a pure speech is related to speech with no anger (1:19–21) and continues under discussion in 4:13—5:6 where the author mentions the concept of "boast in arrogance." Again the use of tongue and the moral idea of evil are connected in these chapters.[91] This connects 5:7–11 which is about the encouragement of endurance to 3:1—4:10. Therefore, the proper manner of talking becomes a decisive issue.[92] On the other hand, the exhor-

90. Dibelius, Perkins, Bauckham, Martin, Cheung, Adamson, and Ropes hold this assertion. Taylor, on the other hand, proposes that there is a hooked word σῶμα (2:26/3:2) to connect this passage to chapter two, along with the themes of perfection (2:22/3:2), and there is a distant hook word χαλιναγωγέω (1.26/3:2). James 2:2–4 illustrates the concept of right speaking, and 3:1–12 is the explanation of the further discussion about law and judgment in 2:8–13. Furthermore, both passages 3:13–18 and 4:1–10 serve as transitional passages which link 3:1–12. But this is not in the scope of this essay. We will focus on the topic of speech here (see Dibelius, *James*, 181; Perkins, *First and Second Peter, James, and Jude*, 115; Bauckham, *James*, 204; Adamson, *James*, 138; Ropes, *Critical and Exegetical Commentary*, 226; Taylor, *Text-Linguistic Investigation*, 115; Martin, *James*, 103–4; Cheung and Bauckham, *Genre*, 74).
91. Taylor, *Text-Linguistic Investigation*, 117.
92. Davids, *James*, 181.

tation to seek for wisdom from above recalls the assertion that wisdom comes through prayer in 1:5–8. The idea of wisdom from above (ἄνωθεν σοφία) in 3:17 is also related to every ideal gift from above (πᾶν δώρημα τέλειον ἄνωθέν) in 1:17. In addition, since the perfect gift is equivalent to the word of truth (λόγῳ ἀληθείας) in 1:18 and the implanted word (ἔμφυτον λόγον) in 1:21, we can summarize that wisdom is highly associated with words.[93]

Summary of the Analysis
According to the analysis above, we can see that the content in 3:1—4:10 echoes several passages in the other chapters of James. The major theme of this passage is that wisdom from above is the pivot of controlling the tongue, which will highly influence moral conduct. The real danger of misusing the tongue is that it could describe the values of the world which is evil. In addition, stewarding the creature is one of God's plans for human beings, but the tongue is the place where this power cannot be exercised. James basically provides the reason for controlling the tongue based on the concept of creation, which is related to the essence of human beings, who are created in God's image.[94] The epistle of James does not focus on the idea of the superiority of human beings as was common in the Greek world.[95] The author, however, is talking about the order of creation, which exhibits God's wisdom. True wisdom is a gift from God, who is generous and ungrudging. When people have the correct relationship with God, this wisdom can be found; if the relationship with God is wrong, this person will be full of chaos and disorder in his or her life. To know the order of creation, which manifests the wisdom of God, is one of the means of knowing how to make a correct relationship with God.

---

93. Edgar, *Has God Not Chosen the Poor?* 23.
94. Carson, "James," 1006.
95. Davids, *James*, 144.

Wisdom of Speech—Confucian and Christian

Similarity: The Manner of Speech is Rooted in External Path (tao)

Both Confucius and the author of James believe that speech has a great influence on morality, and both of them seek *tao* ("path") and wisdom as the recipes for learning how to speak. These two traditions observe the orders as the foundation of knowing this *tao* with their own definitions. In Chinese culture, speech is a matter of respecting the social order. The incorrect manners of speaking are regarded as orderless errors. There are three errors that make a person liable in the presence of a man of virtue and station: "they may speak when it does not come to them to speak—this is called rashness. They may not speak when it comes to them to speak—this is called concealment. They may speak without looking at the countenance of their superior—this is called blindness."[96] There is another speech in one of the four books of Confucian schools: according to *The Great Learning*, "[t]hings have their root and their branches. Affairs have their end and their beginning. Knowing which comes first and which comes last, one is already close to *Tao*."[97] Based on the analysis, one can see that in Chinese culture, how one is talking is more important than what is talking about. People need the order from *tao* to learn how to speak, which is to maintain a good social relationship between people.

In Jas 3:1—4:10, a similar concept is mentioned. The tongue is full of deadly poison, which becomes the image of the serpent which brought death. The pollution of the "whole body" results from a lack of control over the tongue. The one who can control the tongue shows the ability to be pure. Interestingly, the wisdom "from above" is also described as pure. In other words, the wisdom from above becomes the key factor to making a person pure.[98] This concept is similar to that in the Chinese culture, meaning that both perspectives believe that one needs to learn a

---

96. Confucius, *Analects*, 16:6.
97. Confucius, *Ta-Hio*, 1.
98. Lockett, *Purity*, 141.

good manner of speaking from external help, either *tao* from Chinese culture or wisdom from about in the Scriptures.

Differences: Creation Order or Social Order
In the Bible, speech is related to the wisdom from above. People who cannot control their tongue are failed sages. The wisdom from above results from friendship with God whereas the wisdom from below shows the friendship with the world.[99] The author emphasizes that the creation story is a teaching instrument and the situation of not being able to control the tongue represents the situation of the fallen creature, which needs to be restored.[100] The further explanation of the relationship between controlling the tongue and creation is that the tongue can be used to bless God and curse those who are made in the likeness of God at the same time. This contradiction manifests the orderless disarray. The illustrations of fruit (3:12) in this passage are examples to show this muddle. They represent an image of mixed kinds, which violates the natural order of things.[101] To steward nature is one of the purposes of God's creative work, and to tame animals is a way to show this ability of human beings.[102] The order of creation is that human beings are created by God to tame the nonhuman creature.[103] Therefore, the wisdom from above, represents order and limits in the creation. The passage in 3:13–18 further indicates solutions to the problem in the previous discussion, and the creation story provides a framework as the foundation for human beings to have a correct relationship with other creatures, which becomes the foundation of ethical doctrine.[104] Not to cross the boundaries between different creatures will become the central focus of one's speeches and conducts. Teachers are those who expose themselves to the danger of "committing a verbal offense" because they are people who

---

99. Johnson, *Brother of Jesus*, 165.
100. Wall, *Community*, 172–73.
101. Lockett, *Purity*, 124–25.
102. Perkins, *First and Second Peter, James, and Jude*, 118.
103. Laws, *Commentary*, 152–53.
104. Martin, *James*, 119; Hartin and Harrington, *James*, 186–87.

give speeches.[105] They have to lead lives that demonstrate their faith in action. Nevertheless, wisdom from above is not an abstract idea or an object to pursue. Welcoming the word of truth is the way (*tao* in the Chinese language) of obtaining the wisdom from above as a gift from God.[106] When the people of God observe these phenomena, they are seeking God, rather than the wisdom in and of itself. In James, the author depicts God as a friend and benefactor. Friendship with God is the condition of receiving wisdom from above. In addition, holding heavenly wisdom will produce insight into manners and knowing how to interact with other people. To sum up, God's wisdom is revealed in the creature, which those who are God's friend will observe carefully. God's people will praise God when they observe the creature on all the earth (Ps 8:1). The friendship with God establishes the possibility of friendship with others,[107] and the first step is to learn how to control one's tongue.

On the other hand, the quest for nature and human beings getting united in Chinese culture deals only with the physical world, not with the metaphysical one, or especially with the relationships between people. For Confucius, intellect and virtue serve as the foundation of understanding destiny.[108] Confucius thinks that no individual can understand the destiny of heaven fully, but what this person can grasp is enough to guide his or her choices.[109] He thought that learning below would be able to penetrate what is above.[110] In addition, *li* is for the worship of heaven, so that different gods may fulfill their duties. Yet when *li* is practiced in the worship of earth, this will result in growth and multiply.[111] The concept of heave in Confucius's system is different from that in the Bible. Although both the Analects and the book of James talk about heaven, heaven does not reveal itself in the former, whereas heaven creates human beings in the

---

105. Dibelius, *James*, 182.
106. Hartin, "'Who Is Wise and Understanding among You?'"
107. Batten, *Friendship*, 176–77.
108. Confucius, *Analects*, 2:4.
109. Yao, *Wisdom in Early Confucian and Israelite Traditions*, 206–207.
110. Confucius, *Analects*, 14:35.
111. Confucius, *Wisdom*, 161–63.

latter (Jas 3:9). Therefore, Confucius asserted that what happens on earth and how to deal with social relationships are more important than talking about heaven. These metaphysical issues cannot become the mainstream of Chinese culture because he said, "[t]he Master would not discuss unusual occurrences, physical strength, disorder, or spirits."[112] This prevents Confucius from seeking universal principles of knowing the order of nature, the order of social relationship, and the order of creation. In other words, the book of James tells readers to know the boundaries between creatures to learn how to speak, whereas the Analects focuses on maintaining a good balance between various social relationships to provide rules for speech.

Conclusion

In this paper, I have introduced the ethical idea of Chinese culture about speech, Confucius's idea in particular, and I also use James 3:1—4:10 as an example to present the concept of talking in the Bible. Both thoughts take speech very seriously. Speaking carefully is one of the traditional virtues in Chinese culture. Chinese people emphasize individual cultivation to drill *li* and *jen* in their relationships with others. To be considerate and to love others are the two pillars of self-training. These two results from social orders between prince and minister, father and son, couples, brothers (sisters), and friends. One of Confucius's students Mengzi said, "between father and son, there should be affection; between sovereign and minister, righteousness; between husband and wife, attention to their separate functions; between old and young, a proper order; and between friends, fidelity."[113] The satisfactory aspect of social order, which is the key to grasp this wisdom, is to make people fit in Nature.[114] To control the tongue is also an important issue in the Scriptures. From Jas 3:1—4:10, we can observe the idea of speaking carefully as well.

---

112. Confucius, *Analects*, 7:21.
113. Shi, *Meng Zi Jin Zhu Jin Yi*, 31.
114. This idea is from Xunzi, who was one of Confucius's followers (see Ivanhoe, "Values").

The major difference, however, is that these two traditions set up different points of departure. Confucius's approach starts from the bottom and remains among human beings. Natural laws only serve as a mirror for people to learn how to exercise social order. Many Chinese people may have established their theology based on this understanding and pay too much attention to the social relationship but neglect the wisdom from above. God plays a less important role in these people's minds, but to maintain harmony between people becomes their central concern. In the Bible, we discern different access. It begins with God and then moves to people. Chinese culture is horizontal, whereas Christianity is more vertical. Chinese philosophy focuses on social standards and pushes them from the outside toward the inside. Yet Christianity emphasizes the relationship with God which sets up a new life internally which will appear in the interaction between people externally. It is a pity that modern people often neglect the power of speech which held a great influence, for both good and bad.[115] As students of the Bible, we should learn the way to talk which God expects us to use. God is the one who orders creation. Christians inherit this task to set up orders of doing good in our lives, which should be involved in God's "creating and redeeming purposes."[116] The more we understand the wisdom of creation, the more we can control our tongues and use them to bless instead of a curse. From the conclusion of this paper, we may start learning how to speak properly, politely, and wisely. Confucius's model provides many good patterns of *li and jen*, and God's word gives us the real motivation to make them come true in our daily lives. Therefore, people who have been influenced by Confucius's model need to turn their eyes from the social relationships to the relationship between God and human beings (or all creature). In this case, an appropriate manner of speech can be found, and the true harmony among creatures can be maintained because every creature lives after its kind.

---

115. Bauckham, *James*, 204.
116. Long, *Goodness of God*, 280.

Bibliography

Adamson, James B. *James: The Man and His Message*. Grand Rapids: Eerdmans, 1989.

Ames, Roger T. "Thinking through Comparisons: Analytical and Narrative Methods for Cultural Understanding." In *Early China/Ancient Greece: Thinking through Comparisons*, edited by Steven Shankman and Stephen W. Durrant, 93–110. Albany, NY: State University of New York Press, 2002.

Batten, Alicia J. *Friendship and Benefaction in James*. Emory Studies in Early Christianity 15. Blanford Forum, UK: Deo, 2010.

Bauckham, Richard. *James: Wisdom of James, Disciple of Jesus the Sage*. New Testament Readings. New York: Routledge, 1999.

Bo, Chen. "The Debate on the Yan-Yi Relation in Chinese Philosophy: Reconstruction and Comments." *Frontiers of Philosophy in China* 4 (2006) 539–60.

Brown, Gillian, and George Yule. *Discourse Analysis*. New York: Cambridge University Press, 1983.

Carson, D. A. "James." In *Commentary on the New Testament Use of the Old Testament*, edited by G. K. Beale and D. A. Carson, 997–1014. Grand Rapids: Baker, 2007.

Chen, Da Qi, *Kong Xue Lun Ji*. Taipei: Chinese Culture and Publishing Committee, 1957.

Cheung, Luck L., and Richard Bauckham. *The Genre, Composition and Hermeneutics of the Epistle of James*. Paternoster Biblical and Theological Monographs. Carlisle: Paternoster, 2003.

Confucius. *The Analects*. Translated by Arthur Waley. Beijing: Foreign Language Teaching and Research, 1998.

———. *The Analects: Sayings of Confucius*. Translated by D. C. Lau. Harmondsworth, UK: Penguin, 1998.

———. *Ta-Hio: The Great Learning of Confucius*. Translated by Ezra Pound. New Directions Pamphlets 4. Norfolk, CT: New Directions, 1939.

———. *The Wisdom of Confucius*, edited and translated by Yutang Lin et al. New York: Modern Library, 1938.

Cua, A. S. "The Possibility of Ethical Knowledge." In *Epistemological Issues in Classical Chinese Philosophy*, edited by Hans Lenk and Gregor Paul, 159–80. SUNY Series in Chinese Philosophy and Culture. Albany, NY: State University of New York Press, 1993.

Dawson, Miles Menander. *The Ethics of Confucius*. New York: G. P. Putnam's Sons, 1915.

Davids, Peter H. *James*. San Francisco: Harper & Row, 1983.

Defoort, Carine. "Confucius and the 'Rectification of Names': Hu Shi and the Modern Discourse on Zhengming." *Dao: A Journal of Comparative Philosophy* 20 (2021) 613–33.

Dibelius, Martin. *James: A Commentary on the Epistle of James*, edited by Helmut Koester. Translated by Michael A. Williams. Hermenia. Philadelphia: Fortress, 1976.

Edgar, David Hutchinson. *Has God Not Chosen the Poor? The Social Setting of the Epistle of James*. Sheffield: Sheffield Academic, 2001.

English, Adam C. *Theology Remixed: Christianity as Story, Game, Language, Culture.* Downers Grove, IL: InterVarsity, 2010.

Frisina, Warren G. "Ritual: The Root of Trust." *Dao: A Journal of Comparative Philosophy* 20 (2021) 667–73.

Givón, Talmy. *On Understanding Grammar.* Orlando: Academic, 1979.

Gorman, Michael J. *Elements of Biblical Exegesis: A Basic Guide for Students and Ministers.* Peabody, MA: Hendrickson, 2001.

Hartin, P. J. "'Who Is Wise and Understanding among You?' (James 3:13): An Analysis of Wisdom, Eschatology, and Apocalypticism in the Letter of James." In *Conflicted Boundaries in Wisdom and Apocalypticism*, edited by Benjamin G. Wright and Lawrence M. Wills, 149–68. Atlanta: Society of Biblical Literature, 2005.

Hartin, P. J., and Daniel J. Harrington. *James.* Sacra Pagina 14. Collegeville, MN: Liturgical, 2003.

Ivanhoe, Pholop J. "The Values of Spontaneity." In *Taking Confucian Ethics Seriously: Contemporary Theories and Applications*, edited by Kam-por Yu, Julia Tao, and Philip J. Ivanhoe, 183–207. SUNY Series in Chinese Philosophy and Culture. Albany, NY: State University of New York Press, 2010.

Jiang, Meng Lin. "Kongzi Xue Shuo Yu Zhong Guo Wen Hua." In *Kong Xue Jiang Yi*, edited by Chen Ying Dong. Taipei: Zong Guo Li Yue Xue Huei, 1983.

Johnson, Luke Timothy. *Brother of Jesus, Friend of God: Studies on the Letter of James.* Grand Rapids: Eerdmans, 2004.

Junren, Wan. "Reasons for an Easy Access of Christianity into Chinese Culture: Cultural Relativity between Religion and Morality on the Basis of the Method of Matteo Ricci's Missionary Work in China." In *Christianity and Chinese Culture*, edited by Miikka Ruokanen and Paulos Huang, 85–101. Grand Rapids: Eerdmans, 2010.

Lao-Tzu, *The Teachings of Lao-Tzu: The Tao Te Ching*. Translated by Paul Carus. New York: Thomas Dunne, 2000.

Laws, Sophie. *Commentary on the Epistle of James*. Harper's New Testament Commentaries. San Francisco: Harper & Row, 1980.

Liu, Chiaen. "What a Story Is about: Cohesion Analysis of Narrative Topic in Mark 2:1–12." *Chinese Evangelical Seminary Journal* 11 (2020) 30–52.

Lockett, Darian R. *Purity and Worldview in the Epistle of James*. Library of New Testament Studies 336. London: T. & T. Clark, 2008.

Long, D. Stephen. *The Goodness of God: Theology, Church, and the Social Order*. Grand Rapids: Brazos, 2001.

Louw, J. P., and Eugene A. Nida. *Greek–English Lexicon of the New Testament: Based on Semantic Domains*. 2nd ed. 2 vols. New York: United Bible Societies, 1989.

Martin, John Michael. "Understanding the Confucian Analects: Tu Wei-Ming Speaks in Bradley Lecture Series." *Library of Congress Information Bulletin*. Online: https://www.loc.gov/item/prn-98-014/tu-wei-ming-discusses-the-analects-of-confucius/1998-02-03.

Martin, Ralph P. *James*. Word Biblical Commentary 48. Waco, TX: Word, 1988.

Moo, Douglas J. *James: An Introduction and Commentary*. Downers Grove, IL: InterVarsity, 2015.

Nan, Huai Jin. *Lun Yu Yu Kongzi De Xue Shu Si Xiang You Ming Kong Xue Xin Yu*. Taipei: Youth Daily News, 1969.

Perkins, Pheme. *First and Second Peter, James, and Jude*. Interpretation. Louisville: John Knox, 1995.

Porter, Stanley E. "Cohesion in James: A Response to Martin Dibelius." In *The Epistle of James: Linguistic Exegesis of An Early Christian Letter*, edited by James D. Dvorak and Zackary K. Dawson, 45–68. Linguistic Exegesis of the New Testament 1. Eugene, OR: Pickwick, 2019.

———. *Idioms of the Greek New Testament*. 2nd ed. Sheffield: Sheffield Academic, 1999.

Qian, Mu. *Kong Zi Yu Lun Yu*. Taipei: Linking, 1985.

Reed, Jeffrey T. *A Discourse Analysis of Philippians: Method and Rhetoric in the Debate over Literary Integrity*. Journal for the Study of the New Testament Supplement Series 136. Sheffield: Sheffield Academic, 1997.

Ropes, James Hardy. *A Critical and Exegetical Commentary on the Epistle of St James*. International Critical Commentary 39. Edinburgh: T. & T. Clark, 1916.

Rudd, H. F. *Chinese Moral Sentiments before Confucius: A Study in the Origin of Ethical Valuations*. Shanghai: Christian Literature Society Depot, 1915.

Shi, Ci Yun, *Meng Zi Jin Zhu Jin Yi*. Taipei: Commercial, 1995.

Song, Tian Zheng. *Zhong Yong Jin Zhu Jin Yi*. Taipei: Commercial, 1985.

Stoddard, Sally E. *Text and Texture: Patterns of Cohesion*. Advances in Discourse Processes 40. Norwood, NJ: Ablex, 1991.

Taylor, Charles. *Sources of the Self: The Making of the Modern Identity*. Cambridge, MA: Harvard University Press, 1989.

Taylor, Mark Edward. *A Text-Linguistic Investigation into the Discourse Structure of James*. Library of New Testament Studies 311. London: T. & T. Clark, 2006.

Varner, William. *The Book of James: A New Perspective: A Linguistic Commentary Applying Discourse Analysis*. The Woodlands, TX: Kress Biblical Resource, 2010.

———. *James: Evangelical Exegetical Commentary*. Bellingham, WA: Lexham, 2014.

Wall, Robert W. *Community of the Wise: The Letter of James*. The New Testament in Context. Valley Forge, PA: Trinity Press International, 1997.

Westfall, Cynthia Long. "The Analysis of Prominence in Hellenistic Greek." In *The Linguist as Pedagogue: Trends in the Teaching and Linguistic Analysis of the Greek New Testament*, edited by Stanley E. Porter and Matthew Brook O'Donnell, 75–94. New Testament Monographs 11. Sheffield: Sheffield Academic, 2009.

———. "Blessed Be the Ties that Bind Semantic Domains in Hebrew 1:1—4:16." Paper presented at the Theological Research Seminar, McMaster Divinity College, Hamilton, ON, Canada, November 2005.

———. *A Discourse Analysis of the Letter to the Hebrews: The Relationship between Form and Meaning*. Library of New Testament Studies 297. London: T. & T. Clark, 2005.

———. "Mapping the Text: How Discourse Analysis Helps Reveal the Way through James." In *The Epistle of James: Linguistic Exegesis of An Early Christian Letter*, edited by James D. Dvorak and Zackary K. Dawson, 11–44. Linguistic Exegesis of the New Testament 1. Eugene, OR: Pickwick, 2019.

Wong, Yuk. *Ju Chia Ti Chung Ho Kuan*. Hong Kong: Longman, 1967.

Yang, Liang Gong. *Kong Xue Si Lun*. Taipei: Linking, 1983.

Yao, Xinzhong. *Wisdom in Early Confucian and Israelite Traditions*. Ashgate World Philosophies Series. Farnham, UK: Ashgate, 2007.

WISDOM OF WATER

Brad Davis[1]
Putnam, CT, USA

Ever seeking the lowest place
and, though the Quinebaug flows north

before south, never upwardly
mobile, never not for both

alewife and osprey, unborn and mother.
When rapid beyond class two,

it is not the water that's to blame
but the channel, what below

the uninviting surface threatens.
For water receives a body without

condition or censure, and who wouldn't
want to be gracious as water,

as what falls on every last body that lies
beneath what has risen above?

---

1. Brad Davis is the author of four full-length poetry collections, including *Trespassing on the Mount of Olives* (2021, Poiema/Cascade) and *On the Way to Putnam: new, selected, & early poems* (2024, Grayson Books). Canadian from birth, he has lived most of his life in the United States, and recently, to honor his British Columbian mother, he received the official certificate from Ottawa affirming his life-long Canadian citizenship.

INDEFECTIBLE (THE WORD)

You may or may not want
this to describe your life,
but if you're anything like me
and this is your first time
hearing the word *indefectible*,

then likely you're debating
either to retrieve your phone
and do a search for it or
to relax into a more intuitive
pose and wait for a sense

of the word's meaning to rise
from the good earth of context.
I'm not going to give it away,
but I will say it cannot be
said of you. And just in case

you picture me gloating,
the indefectible life being mine,
rest assured, neither can it
be said of me. What I can
do is point you to an ancient

Latinism crafted by Augustine
of Hippo—*non posse peccare*—
that describes what life is not
now, but may, come the Day
and forever thereafter, come to be.

TIME, DON'T COME FOR ME

Maya Venters[1]
Canada

At times, I have a second,
a split in pace, two fractured
minds which cannot be reckoned.
One space, manufactured
by some impulse to keep
the clock, the other, stock
of memories which creep
out from their key and lock.
Sometimes, I need a minute
as I pull one side from
another. There's a limit
to thought, to truth; we succumb
to madness and beget
realities askew.
Time, don't come for me yet,
I still have much to do.

---

1. Maya is a Canadian writer and MFA candidate at the University of St. Thomas (TX). Her chapbook *Life Cycle of a Mayfly* won the Vallum Chapbook Prize. She has published in *The Literary Review of Canada*, *Modern Age*, and *Rattle*, among others. Maya can be found at https://mayaventers.ca.

GATEKEEPERS

This gate we keep will rust
and fall off broken hinges.
And when we turn to dust,
to dust this gate shall go.
So all this too, shall pass,
but each seed we once sowed
behind this gate will last,
return each spring, regrow.

BEAVER POND

I saw him once. Between two quiet moments
when everything was cloaked in the warm sun-
fade and the haze of frog song by the pond.
He pierced the surface like a finger in
an open wound, leaving a wake behind
him big enough to haul a bright new world.
Since then, I haven't seen him. Maybe I
scared him away, or maybe he has changed
his route for fear of his disrupting me.
But still, at every turn, I look for him.
I'm left unsatisfied by that first glimpse
and go on hungrily searching for another.
Something about his presence reassures me.
I yearn to know that "Beaver Pond" is not
some teasing name a child once gave this place,
attracting false hope with a camera round
its neck. And so I wait along this bank.
I cannot see the dam. I cannot swim.
I'm subject only to the ebb and flow
of faith with every unrevealing ripple.
But even so, each night as my mind wanders
through all the violence that one life can bear
and must go on rebearing till it ends,

I hear a splash come through the open window
and think the beaver must be out there still:
kicking beneath the surface, rising sometimes
to meet the sun, his toothy smile expanding
into eternity. I guess that I
should know, for once he let me catch a glimpse.

SPIRITUAL INSIGHT IN THE WORKS OF HENRY O. TANNER

Erin Wildsmith
Highview Community Church, St Marys, ON

Introduction: An Artistic Encounter

In a first encounter with a work of art, there is a sense in which it stands on its own, independent of its history and origins. We encounter it as if it exists *out there* in the world, without the artist standing nearby to offer explanation or justification. In this manner, it remains subjective and malleable, changing subtly as it interacts with each viewer's perspective, context, and history. It was in this fashion, independent and cut off from its source, that I first encountered the splendid painting *The Annunciation* by Henry Ossawa Tanner (1859–1937).

I was particularly drawn to the expression and body language of young Mary, as Tanner has rendered her, in the very moment of receiving the angel's wonderful and terrible message, "You will conceive and will give birth to a son" (Luke 1:31, NIV). The delicate combination of fear and courage in Tanner's Mary has deepened my own Advent reflections every year since I first encountered it. I have also been moved to share this work with my congregation in hopes of strengthening their faith with Tanner's fresh take on a familiar Bible story. Such is the potency of a piece of art that is left to *speak for itself*. Yet this power also comes at a price.

To strip a work of art from its history from the hands that formed it and the life that led to its creation is to see it only imperfectly, that is, from a limited perspective. One is left with the subjective effect of the work but robbed of its substance. When the history and life of the artist are revealed, the work may lose some of the evocative power of an initial encounter, yet it also takes on new depth and significance, or rather, the inherent depth and significance within are revealed. This was my experience when I learned about the life of the exceptional nineteenth-century American artist Henry Ossawa Tanner. Encountering Tanner's history and some of his other paintings, including *The Banjo Lesson*, *The Raising of Lazarus*, and *Daniel in the Lion's Den*, gave me a new appreciation for this international artist and the spiritual power of his work. It is my belief that Tanner's work has the potential to greatly enrich the Christian spiritual journey through his fresh interpretations of biblical scenes, but also for his complex portrayal of the human subjects of his work. It is my contention that the emotional nuance and sensitivity of Tanner's work has potential to deepen our understanding not only of the stories, but of ourselves as well.

The Early Life of Henry O. Tanner

Henry Ossawa Tanner was born in 1859 to parents Benjamin Tucker Tanner and Sarah Miller Tanner. As most parents do, they named their son with utmost care, choosing his middle name, Ossawa, as a nod to abolitionist John Brown and his defiant anti-slavery actions taken at Osawatomie, Kansas in 1856.[1] Henry's parentage and even his name embedded him in a centuries long struggle against racism and prejudice Black Americans continued to face in the years following the abolition of slavery in the US. This was a struggle that Henry would continue to face even as his artistic skill became increasingly apparent and as he sought to distinguish himself as an artist in his own right.

Henry's father Benjamin Tanner was a well-known preacher in the African Methodist Episcopalian (AME) church and a man of considerable intelligence and dignity. He developed a reputation as an advocate for racial justice one hundred years before the Civil Rights movement. The words of Benjamin Tanner from his journal exemplify his frustration regarding the double standard to which coloured people were regularly subjected:

---

1. Woods, *Henry Ossawa Tanner*, x.

> If the colored people would only do right is the cry from the parlor to the kitchen, from the Senate Hall to the country squire shanty. "Colored people won't do right." Right, what do they mean by right, is it to see while yet their eyes have been put out, to love labor while yet they are taught none but the meanest work—to love their country, while yet it brands them the most infamous on earth. To love their race while yet from infancy they are taught to believe their natural inferiority. If colored people would do right. Oh yes, to do that "right" we would not be men.[2]

This maddening labyrinth of stereotypes and unjust laws created the backdrop for Henry Tanner's early life and would have a significant impact on his career as an artist.[3]

Tanner later recalled the exact moment he realized that he wanted to become an artist. As an adult he recounted one day as an adolescent boy where he observed an artist painting a landscape out of doors. Though the thought of pursuing art had not previously crossed his mind, Tanner became so fascinated watching the artist work that he knew at that moment that he had found his life's vocation. He said,

> It was this simple event that, as it were, set me on fire. Like many children, I had drawn upon my slate to the loss of my lessons, or all over the fences to the detriment of the landscape; but never had it crossed my mind that I should be an artist, nor had I even wished to be. But, after seeing this artist at work for an hour, it was decided on the spot, by me at least, that I would be one, and I assure you it was no ordinary one I had in mind.[4]

His decision made, the young Tanner set out in search of a teacher. But here too he encountered the ever-present burden of racial prejudice.[5] Eventually, Tanner succeeded in obtaining admission to the Philadelphia Academy of Fine Arts (PAFA) where he grew in skill, and his talent became more readily apparent. Yet even among his artistic peers, Tanner could not escape the sting of racist notions and the inability of some of his class-

---

2. Woods, *Henry Ossawa Tanner*, 10.
3. Woods, *Henry Ossawa Tanner*, 6.
4. Woods, *Henry Ossawa Tanner*, 17.
5. Woods, *Henry Ossawa Tanner*, 3.

mates to tolerate being superseded in their skills by a Black classmate. In later years, Tanner would recount the pain he experienced as a result of the persistent racism at PAFA including one unpleasant incident in which Tanner was tied to his easel.[6] Though every bit as talented as his White peers, the ubiquitous stigma and prejudice Tanner faced in America became too much, eventually leading him to pursue his career in Paris, where he did not face the same barriers to recognition and respect within his field that he encountered at home.

American Racism and International Acclaim

Tanner thrived in Paris and for the most part, seemed to enjoy his life and work unencumbered by the barriers imposed at home. Tanner had long made his desire known to be taken seriously as an artist, on his own terms. Reflecting on the relief he experienced in Paris following many difficult experiences in America, Tanner commented, "In Paris, no one regards me curiously. I am simply an American artist. Nobody knows or cares what was the complexion of my forebearers. I live and work there on terms of equality."[7] It was also in Paris where Tanner's work obtained a level of recognition that had eluded him in the US. It was here that he achieved honourable mention at the prestigious salon in 1896 for *Daniel in the Lion's Den* and then a third-place medal a year later for *The Resurrection of Lazarus*.[8]

Tanner's relationship with his racial identity is an item of much interest to many who engage with his work, even to this day. Despite his desire that he be evaluated solely on the basis of his skill and his work, Tanner, a light-skinned Black man, was often the subject of intense debate as fans and critics alike sought to locate him in arbitrary racial categories. To this day, when Tanner's work is mentioned, one finds discussions not only of his racial location but also of his views of this location. Some argue that when Tanner grew tired of the constant prejudice and

6. "On our Cover," 259.
7. Woods, "Henry Ossawa Tanner's Negotiation," 890.
8. Woods, "Henry Ossawa Tanner's Negotiation," 896.

harassment, he tried to distance himself from his racial identity. Yet Tanner scholar Naurice Woods rejects this view, asserting that the words and actions of Tanner which have been so interpreted by others, express less a denial of ethnic heritage than a level of exasperation with arbitrary race classifications which reinforced prejudice and failed to get to the heart of the matter, Tanner's considerable artistic acumen.[9]

Tanner's choice of subject matter has also not escaped the issue of race. While there was a time early in his career when Tanner depicted scenes of Black domestic life such as *The Banjo Lesson* and *The Grateful Poor*, he made a decisive shift upon his relocation to Paris and began depicting biblical scenes instead.[10] While this shift in focus may have been disappointing to some, particularly from his own ethnic community,[11] it was not such a divergence from Tanner's roots as it may seem. Tanner was, after all, a preacher's son, and his shift toward biblical scenes was an exploration of another part of his identity as he depicted visually and powerfully the same stories he had heard in his father's sermons all his life. Taken as a whole, Tanner's body of work explores complex themes including race, faith, and human emotion, and as such, can provide valuable resources for the Christian journey. The remaining sections of this paper will reflect on four of Tanner's paintings, their subjects, themes, style, and how each might serve as resources for theological reflection.

The Banjo Lesson: *Black Dignity and Generational Learning*

The Banjo Lesson is one of the Tanner paintings which audiences seem to find most captivating, partially because it is one of the very few he created depicting Black domestic life. Throughout his career, Tanner expressed great frustration at his inability to escape the issue of race in his work. While he experienced some reprieve during his time in Paris, back home, Tanner's

9. Woods, "Henry Ossawa Tanner's Negotiation," 888.
10. Boime, "Subversion of Genre," 415.
11. Boime, "Subversion of Genre," 415.

work was constantly qualified by the introduction of artificial race categories. Sometimes this conversation of Tanner's ethnic heritage came from the White journalists or art critics, but other times, it was members of the Black community who pinned on Tanner their hopes to break free from stereotypes imposed by the broader White society.[12]

The Banjo Lesson
Henry Ossawa Tanner, 1893 (Oil on canvas)

The Banjo Lesson depicts a small boy seated on the knee of an elderly Black man, perhaps his grandfather, as the older man carefully shows the young boy how to make the chords. The scene is tender and simple yet subversive in its own way as it pushes against the stereotypes of the day. Even in reconstructionist America, the nation was very far from recognizing the full humanity of its Black citizens. Many prejudices and caricatures of

---

12. "On our Cover," 261.

the Black person existed, among them was the image of Black person minstrel: naturally jolly and imbued with innate musical ability that was more instinct than skill. As Tanner portrays them, both the boy and the old man are focused on their task, paying careful attention to the placement of the boy's fingers on the strings as he is helped by the older man to form the notes. The scene radiates the focus and attentive teaching of a master and his student.

The Banjo Lesson was exactly the type of image that many Civil Rights activists were hoping that Tanner would continue to produce, since they provided a viable alternative to and polemic against many of the racist depictions of Blacks in art at the time.[13] However, this was not to be. Having relocated to Paris, Tanner began and continued to paint primarily biblical scenes. The reason for this is unknown. Perhaps this shift represents just another period of Tanner's artistic development and shifting of interests, the likes of which he had undergone before.[14] Perhaps, as some have suggested, Tanner moved away from portraits of Black domestic life because there was simply no market for them in Paris, and he was as bound by the need to put food on the table as any artist. Whatever the reason, *The Banjo Lesson* remains one of a few gems we now have by which to admire this side of such a talented artist. Although this piece does not depict a biblical story or explicitly religious theme, *The Banjo Lesson* offers viewers the opportunities to reflect on spiritual realities of human existence.

When one observes this piece, it is the humanity of the older man and the small boy which grab the viewer's attention. Tanner painted his subjects with immense sympathy, accurately and portraying the tender and powerful relationship that can exist between grandparents and grandchildren and the value of passing on family skills and wisdom to the next generation. Reflecting on this piece can help the viewer call to mind the centrality of relationships in the formation of human identity, a truth perhaps even more urgent in our individualistic western context.

13. "On our Cover," 261.
14. "On our Cover," 261.

The truth is that we are who we are in the context of relationships, and we know what we know because at some point, someone taught it to us. Scripture calls us to give due respect to the familial relationships in which we are embedded, honouring our parents (Exod 20:12) and treating elders with respect (1 Tim 5:1). In its own day, *The Banjo Lesson* served as a needed reminder of the shared humanity of all people. It still serves us in this way, even as it draws our attention to the power of human relationships with its potent reminder that to love and to be loved really is what life is all about.

The Resurrection of Lazarus: *Encountering the Divine*

Though criticized by some, Tanner's artistic shift toward biblical scenes left a significant impression on many in the art world and beyond. Tanner's biblical paintings are well known for the emotional complexity displayed by his subjects. Although not a title he took upon himself, Tanner has been called a visual mystic by some for the powerful ability of his work to help viewers encounter the stories, and perhaps even God in new and unique ways.[15]

Among his biblical masterpieces, *The Resurrection of Lazarus*, currently housed at the Museé D'Orsay in Paris, earned him considerable recognition and acclaim when it was first purchased by the French government for the Musée du Luxembourg in 1897.[16] Among its other merits, *The Resurrection of Lazarus* demonstrates Tanner's skill at portraying the complexity and nuance of human emotion. The scene is familiar for those who know the Bible, depicting the narrative from John 11 where Jesus raises Lazarus from the dead. The story itself is rife with tension and emotional complexity, which Tanner captures extraordinarily well. The figures in the background portray a variety of reactions to what has just transpired from fear, exhibited by the figure covering their face, to wonder like the woman beside Jesus who looks intently in his direction. The man in the

---

15. Baker, "Henry Ossawa Tanner," 32.
16. "On our Cover," 161.

background seems to be expressing praise to God for what he has just witnessed with hands raised up in praise, while the figures further in the background simply watch in silent astonishment.

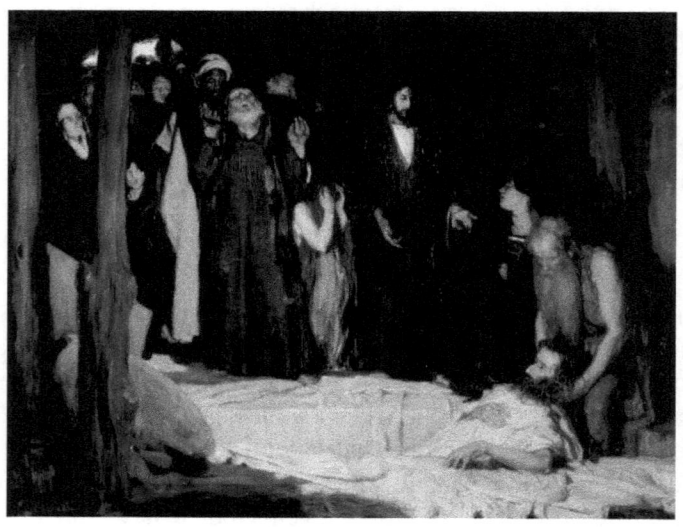

The Resurrection of Lazarus
Henry Ossawa Tanner, 1896 (Oil on canvas)

Both Jesus and Lazarus have expressions that are more difficult to read. Jesus appears calm, almost relaxed as he stands over Lazarus's grave, hands outstretched. Lazarus, for his part, seems mostly confused. He is reminiscent of a person who has awoken abruptly from sleeping and is not yet entirely cognizant or aware of what is happening. He seems to exist somewhere between death and life, though his left hand, fingers pushing up against the ground, with an active bend in the wrist, as well as his posture, a clear movement from laying down to sitting up, makes it clear to the viewer that that his trajectory is firmly in the direction of life.

The Resurrection of Lazarus has moved art lovers for over a hundred years with its engaging portrayal of this beloved story. Yet it also offers great potential as a resource for theological reflection within the Christian community even beyond its obvious aesthetic appeal. Catherine Abell observes that representational art works possess three kinds of content: explicit representational content, conveyed content (related to all that is implicit in the work), and expressive content, which is concerned primarily with the portrayal of mental states.[17] It is Tanner's mastery of both the conveyed and expressive content of *The Resurrection of Lazarus* that contribute to its impact.

The expressive content in *The Resurrection of Lazarus* is evident in the wide range of emotions which this painting contains in its figures. Taken together, these varied responses seem to capture something of the ambivalence human beings experience toward the work of God. The Lord says through the prophet Isaiah "my thoughts are not your thoughts" (Isa 55:8, NIV). Indeed, the dissonance between how God acts and how human beings experience those actions is often pronounced. Even in the case of raising a man from the dead, an event that would seem unequivocally positive, human beings have a limited ability to absorb the new reality. The varied responses of the people in this painting show this clearly. And yet, importantly, all these people with all their reactions, all they understand or fail to understand about what they have seen, all find their place in the presence of Jesus. As a resource for theological reflection *The Resurrection of Lazarus* is an invitation to *come as you are*.

Whether we are ready or not, full of faith or not, we are invited by Tanner in this painting to simply come and see what God has done. This invitation is at the very heart of the Christian gospel. God is ever doing something powerful and human beings are invited, as the shepherds were, to simply go and bear witness. This is a message the world desperately needs to hear and sometimes it is preached most powerfully without any words at all.

The Annunciation: *Expressionism and Emotional Complexity*

Among the masterpieces of Henry Ossawa Tanner, *The Annunciation*, painted in 1898 stands out as a stark example of the artist's use of detail, subtlety, and understatement to great effect.

---

17. Abell, "Expression in the Representational Arts," 23.

This scene depicts the virgin Mary on the day she is visited by the angel Gabriel to receive news that would ultimately impact not only her own life, but all human history. Art lovers and critics alike have remarked on Tanner's expert ability to portray the complexity of this moment for Mary.

The Annunciation
Henry Ossawa Tanner, 1898 (Oil on canvas)

In an exhibition of the painting at the Worchester Art Museum in February 2019, curator Erin Corrales-Diaz remarked on the uniqueness of Tanner's interpretation of Mary in this moment among the scores of other portrayals of this scene in Western art. Unlike many other paintings which depict the virgin as stately, ethereal, and even somewhat stoic as she receives the angel's words, Tanner has cast her as an awkward teenager, displaying an obvious youth and naivete along with a delicate mix of curiosity and anxiety.[18] Tanner had spent time in the Holy Land and the evidence of this also shows up in the painting.

---

18. Sullivan, "Forgotten Pioneer," para. 12.

Mary's garments as well as the tapestries and rug which can be seen in her bedroom are all consistent with the types of fabric Tanner had encountered in his travels, adding to the painting's authenticity.

Another unique feature of Tanner's version of this scene comes from his portrayal of the angel Gabriel, not—as he is often depicted—with a human appearance augmented by halo and wings but as a streak of bright white light to the left of the piece. Corrales-Diaz notes, "in the late 19th century, electricity was seen as 'miraculous and spectacular' . . . which may be why Tanner portrayed this divine force radiating like a lightning bolt."[19] Whatever the motivation for this artistic choice, the effects are striking.

Using the lens of expression theory, we would understand the presence of Gabriel to be part of the conveyed content of the work, his presence implicit rather than explicit. This artistic choice makes his presence in the painting more impactful in modern times. It is exceedingly difficult to portray angels or other divine encounters in ways that do not tip them over the edge into the trite or the absurd, as a winged and haloed figure is bound to do. The flash of light and how it reflects off the room as well as Mary's face reveals that something significant is happening, even as the details of the divine messenger remain obscured. As with *The Resurrection of Lazarus*, it is Tanner's great skill in capturing human emotion that seems to recommend *The Annunciation* not only as a great painting, but as a resource for theological reflection which could be of great value to the Christian church.

Mary's face in particular gives us pause. She is clearly afraid, whether of the angel himself or of the message he brings we cannot be certain, but having read and familiarized ourselves with the story, we know her famous response, "I am the Lord's servant, may it be to me as you have said" (Luke 1:38, NIV). There is much to be gained from meditating on Mary's example that fear and courage are not mutually exclusive. Certainly, there are

---

19. Sullivan, "Forgotten Pioneer," para. 17.

other ways to express this idea, sermons, for instance. But in the same way we search the faces and body language of others to discern such subtle cues as interest, discomfort, consent, or love, so Tanner's Mary preaches to us many eloquent sermons through her physical response to the divine: full of bravery that will move the world, even while she remains very much afraid.

Daniel in the Lion's Den: *Two Sides to Every Story*

Although Henry O. Tanner produced many works that would be well used as resources for the spiritual life, the last we shall consider for the purposes of this paper is his enigmatic piece *Daniel in the Lion's Den*. In "On our Cover," *The Journal of Nineteenth Century Americanists* observes that while Tanner's art went through several phases over the course of his career, including animals, shipwrecks, landscapes, scenes of Black domestic life and finally biblical scenes, lions remained an enduring interest and show up repeatedly throughout.[20]

Daniel in the Lion's Den
Henry Ossawa Tanner, 1907–1918 (Oil on Canvas)

20. "On our Cover," 161.

Daniel in the Lion's Den has an interesting history. The original painting was painted in 1896 but was lost, with the later version having been created in 1918.[21] Some art historians have supposed that Tanner's Daniel, originally painted during the Dreyfus Affair, was intended to symbolize the French government's unfair treatment of Dreyfus, and further, to emphasize the similarities between the racism which the French government was exhibiting in their dealings with Dreyfus and its American cousin which caused Tanner to relocate in order to pursue his vocation in peace.[22] Whether Tanner intended this or not, his interpretation of the story in this impressionistic piece was certainly unusual.

The biblical account is fraught with tension. Having been duped by his advisors, King Darius finds himself with no choice but to throw Daniel, his favourite staff member, into the lion's den. The narrator of the book of Daniel draws out the scene to maximize the feeling of unease. Darius cannot eat that night, nor does he desire any entertainment and through the long night, he cannot sleep (Dan 6:16–18). Tanner's interpretation of Daniel's experience is striking in contrast to how the scene is often portrayed. The narrator places great emphasis on the fear experienced by King Darius, and as readers we share his fear. Yet the text makes no mention that Daniel was afraid. Tanner's Daniel does not seem afraid, and what is perhaps even more noteworthy, the lions do not seem even remotely interested in eating him.[23] Instead, they seem to walk about his feet, showing only mild interest as if they were a collection of stray cats in some back alley and not a den of (presumably) hungry lions whose express purpose was to devour enemies of the state.

Through the lens of expressionism,[24] it is intriguing to consider the conveyed content of Tanner's *Daniel in the Lion's Den*. What is explicit in the piece are the actors in the scene: Daniel

---

21. "On our Cover," 161.
22. "On our Cover," 161.
23. "On our Cover," 162.
24. Expressionism is an aesthetic theory in which art is primarily concerned with the expression of emotion.

and a pack of hungry lions, all of whom have found themselves placed in this situation by others for the purpose of achieving an outcome desired by the others, that is, that Daniel gets eaten. Implicit is the unwillingness of any of the actors to play their assigned roles: the lions refuse to attack Daniel and Daniel rejects the terror he is supposed to feel in favour of a detached calm. *The Journal of Nineteenth Century Americanists* supposes that audiences might consider this stoicism on the face of Daniel as representative of the attitude Tanner himself demonstrated throughout his artistic career.[25] Though cast in many roles by others from the degrading role of *negro* through the lens of American White supremacy, to the role of exemplar and race champion from some in his own community, Tanner remained intent on expressing his own vision as an artist and allowing his work to speak for itself, beyond any of the roles into which others would prefer to cast him.

This piece too offers rich spiritual insight to any who would stop and pay attention. Christians would do well to consider Tanner's unorthodox interpretation of this well-known story and allow it to help them encounter the text with fresh eyes. In a similar way that the Ignatian exercises[26] invite people to place themselves inside a biblical text by conjuring the sights, smells and sounds even casting themselves as characters in the story, so this painting offers a similar invitation to employ the imagination as we experience this text. Are we Daniel, calm, maybe even a little bit bored as we wait for Darius and the others to discover the truth? Are we the officials, giddy with the thought that by morning our rival will be out of the picture? Are we Darius, tormented by his own naivete and weak will which has put Daniel in this situation?

Tanner's *Daniel in the Lion's Den* reminds us to think twice about the stories we have *heard*, whether from the Bible or elsewhere. The story as you have heard it is not necessarily the whole story, or even the story as it really happened. There is much information we do not have access to. This was true for all

---

25. "On our Cover," 163.
26. St. Ignatius, *Spiritual Exercises*.

awaiting Daniel's fate, it was true for White Americans in the nineteenth century who had constructed for themselves a narrative about who could do what, and it is true for us as too. As we live our days on Earth and in the presence of God, we must recognize that, even at our best, we are working with limited information. We best remain humble.

Our Multifaceted Humanity: Tanner's Work as a Resource for the Spiritual Life

The son of a prominent preacher and gifted artist who focused on biblical scenes, many have sought to cast Henry Ossawa Tanner as attempting to achieve with his brush what his father, Benjamin Tucker Tanner achieved through his sermons. Indeed, this was one of many ill-fitting labels thrust upon Tanner throughout his artistic career as various others sought to define the artist for their own purposes. "Visual Preacher" may not have been a title Tanner was willing to own, yet Tanner's paintings are undoubtedly filled with treasures which the patient and observant viewer will discover.

With his nuanced portrayal of human emotion and his fresh interpretation of some of our best-known Bible stories, Tanner's work invites us to consider our multifaceted humanity, including its hidden and difficult dimensions, and encourages us to bring these untidy and subversive parts of ourselves into dialogue with the Divine. He who resisted the labels so many were keen to pin on to him invites us to hear old stories in new ways, and this is precisely the sort of attentiveness Jesus himself encourages us to cultivate as we seek engagement with God in the context of our daily lives.

Bibliography

Abell, Catherine. "Expression in the Representational Arts." *American Philosophical Quarterly* 50 (2013) 23–35.

Baker, Kelly J. "Henry Ossawa Tanner: Race, Religion, and Visual Mysticism." MA thesis, Florida State University, 2008.

"On our Cover: Henry Ossawa Tanner, *Lions in the Desert* (1897)." *J19: The Journal of Nineteenth-Century Americanists* 9 (2021) 259–64. https://doi.org/10.1353/jnc.2021.0024.

St. Ignatius. *The Spiritual Exercises of St. Ignatius*, edited and translated by Louis J. Puhl. Mansfield Center, CT: Martino, 2010.

Sullivan, Mark. "A Forgotten Pioneer." *Telegram & Gazette*, February 2019. No pages. Online: https://www.telegram.com/story/news/local/worcester/2019/02/15/worcester-art-museum-docent-promotes-forgotten-pioneer/5971083007.

Woods, Naurice Frank, Jr. *Henry Ossawa Tanner*: Art, Faith, Race and Legacy. New York: Routledge, 2017.

———. "Henry Ossawa Tanner's Negotiation of Race and Art: Challenging the 'Unknown Tanner.'" *Journal of Black Studies* 42 (2011) 887–905.

"It Takes a While for People's Hearts to Catch Up with Their Heads": Women's Ordination in the Baptist Convention of Ontario and Quebec

Taylor Murray
Tyndale University, Toronto, ON

Leanne Friesen
Canadian Baptists of Ontario and Quebec, Toronto, ON

Introduction

Although many Baptists in Ontario and Quebec today take pride in their denomination's willingness to ordain women, the journey toward the participation and acceptance of female ministers was not a straightforward one.[1] Various historians have noted that the Baptist Convention of Ontario and Quebec (BCOQ) ordained its first woman in 1947, but few recognize that it did not ordain another until 1979.[2] Complicating this legacy further is the fact that the first woman ordained by the BCOQ, Muriel Spurgeon (1922–2023; later Muriel Spurgeon Carder), had no intention of ministering in a Canadian congregation upon ordination, which both made her a relatively inoffensive candidate and ensured that the issue of women's ordination would remain a theoretical question for most Baptists in the region for several decades. Indeed, it was not until years later, when other Evangel-

---

1. In 2008, the Baptist Convention of Ontario and Quebec (BCOQ) changed its name to the Canadian Baptists of Ontario and Quebec (CBOQ). This paper retains this historical usage (BCOQ).

2. E.g., Heath, Friesen, and Murray, *Baptists in Canada*, 72–73; and Brackney, *Baptists in North America*, 241. Notably, Harry Renfree's influential history of Baptists in Canada makes only passing reference to women's ordination (see, e.g., *Heritage and Horizon*, 251) and mentions it only to discuss ordination councils.

icals began to grapple with the issue of women's ordination, that the BCOQ was forced to deal with the issue of women's ordination more tangibly than it had in the past, which resulted in a decision officially to ordain women to active ministry in a church context. These observations complicate the story of women's ordination among Baptists in Ontario and Quebec and show that the BCOQ was much more reticent to accept women's ordination fully than is commonly realized.

The purpose of this article, therefore, is twofold. First, to provide a history of the ordination of women in the BCOQ. The absence of any meaningful description of this event and its aftermath is a significant lacuna in the existing literature. Second, to identify the reasons for the apparent cognitive dissonance between policy and practice that effectively stymied progress for women in the BCOQ for upward of three decades. That there was an extended period of time between these ordinations was not unique to the BCOQ, and, in fact, it reflected the lived reality for women in numerous other denominations as well.[3] Still, this more than three-decade gap raises obvious questions about the attitudes toward women's ordination within BCOQ churches at the time, and it warrants exploration. Similar to what Valerie J. Korinek has documented in her study on women's ordination in the United Church of Canada, while the denomination was willing to ordain women, it does not mean the churches were prepared to accept this practice.[4] To trace this history, this paper begins by exploring early perspectives on women's ordination in the BCOQ before documenting the ordinations in 1947 and 1979 and their individual contexts. Although the BCOQ signalled that it was ready to ordain women as early as the 1940s, this paper shows that it was a qualified acceptance that did not necessarily reflect the larger denominational constituency and was not tangibly ratified for several decades.

---

3. E.g., Maxwell, "'You Can't, 'Cause You're a Girl,'" 62; and Chaves, *Ordaining Women*.

4. Korinek, "No Women Need Apply."

Early Attitudes

During the nineteenth and early twentieth centuries, Baptists in Ontario and Quebec were not unique in their view of the role of women in the church. Across the denominational spectrum in Canada, women were barred from most forms of professional ministry. For many of their male counterparts, there was no ambiguity in the Apostle Paul's admonition: "Let your women keep silence in the churches . . . for it is a shame for women to speak in the church" (1 Cor 14:34–35, KJV).[5] Naturally, this restriction included ordained ministry.[6] Yet, at the same time, by the turn of the twentieth century, women in various Canadian denominations had also managed to carve out a significant place in the life of the church as fundraisers, missionaries, teachers, and activists; and they operated through various societies, auxiliaries, and circles with increasing independence and authority.[7] These changes reflected similar shifts that were occurring in Canadian society during this period, as a greater number of women were beginning to enter the workforce. While the era's cultural expectations still limited what women could or could not do in both church and society at large,[8] opportunities that had once been closed to women were slowly opening. As Judith Colwell sums, it was during this period that "Women moved from anonymity to ex-

---

5. E.g., Joshua Denovan, "Woman's Sphere and Work," *The Canadian Baptist* (15 June 1893), 1.

6. There were notable exceptions, including among Baptists in Canada. Pat Townsend has recently discovered that Reformed Baptists in New Brunswick ordained Ella Kinney Sanders in 1901. Another early example was Jennie Johnson, who was ordained by Free Will Baptists in Michigan in 1909, but spent several years serving in Ontario. These cases were exceptional and anomalous, however, and did not reflect the larger trends in Canadian Christianity. For resources on these figures, see Reid-Maroney, *Reverend Jennie Johnson*; and Mullen, *"I Believe"*, 338–40.

7. For a few important studies on women in Canadian Christianity during this period, see Whiteley, *Canadian Methodist Women*; Cook, *"Through Sunshine and Shadow"*; Gagan, *Sensitive Independence*; and Brouwer, *New Women for God*. Esther Barnes (*Our Heritage*) chronicles the contributions that women made among Baptists in Ontario and Quebec but does not give much attention to the issues described in this article.

8. Strong-Boag, *"Janey Canuck"*, 7–10.

pression of their faith in daily church life that fell just short of actual ordained ministry."[9]

The first documented BCOQ-wide discussion on the ordination of women did not begin until 1929. These discussions were part of a larger trend in Canadian Christianity. During the same period, other denominations grappled with whether or not it was appropriate and theologically permissible to admit women to professional ministry. Among the first was the United Church of Canada, which, only eleven years after forming, opened the ordination process to women in 1936.[10] For their part, the BCOQ entered into discussion on the topic at the annual convention gathering of 1929 when Hugh McDiarmid, a pastor from Toronto, moved that the convention adopt a resolution calling for the establishment of a committee to discuss the issue of women's ordination. The resolution stated,

> Whereas we appreciate the work of womanhood in the varied ministries of the Christian Church; and Whereas several young women have served most acceptably under the appointment of our Home Mission Board; and Whereas we are informed that certain young women of our communion have expressed their purpose to seek a place in the regular pastorate of our churches: Therefore, be it resolved, that while recognizing the right of any local church to call and ordain whom it will, we deem it advisable that, before any such specific case Comes before us, our Convention should pronounce upon the principle of the ordination of women.[11]

According to the resolution, the question of women's ordination had been prompted by several "young women" in the convention who had expressed their interest in ordination. Unfortunately, very little is known about these prospective candidates, but their alleged existence is significant if for no other reason than that it shows that this was a growing concern within the BCOQ in certain circles.

---

9. Colwell, "Role of Women," 51.
10. For an important study on this topic, see Korinek, "No Women Need Apply."
11. MacLeod, ed., *Baptist Year Book for Ontario, Quebec and Western Canada, 1929*, 54, 68.

The resolution's recognition of "the right of any local church to call and ordain whom it will" is also worth noting. The BCOQ's decision to open a discussion on women's ordination should be viewed in its larger context of a significant change that was occurring in the convention at the time: the move to a centralized standing ordination council. Indeed, out of a desire to ensure that Baptist pastors ordained in the convention met a certain level of competency, the BCOQ had introduced plans to institute a standing council, comprised of at least one member from each regional association and whomever else the convention delegates elected.[12] The plan to restructure and ultimately centralize the convention's ordination process required a discussion on the basic requirements for ministry, which included whether the convention would officially open this process to women.

The resolution proceeded to identify possible members who might sit on this proposed committee. Among them were several notable stalwarts of the BCOQ at the time, including R. R. McKay, president of the convention; A. L. McCrimmon, former chancellor of McMaster University; George T. Webb, superintendent of religious education; Jessie E. Zavitz, the president of the Women's Baptist Home Mission Society of Ontario West; Maud Matthews, prominent laywoman and wife of the future Lieutenant Governor of Ontario; H. Edgar Allen from Aylmer; D. D. Gray from Ottawa; and E. D. Lang from Kitchener.[13] It is worth noting the presence of women on the proposed committee. Although clearly outnumbered by men, Zavitz and Matthews provided a feminine voice that was not always present in these kinds of discussions.

As McDiarmid's resolution concluded, it again addressed the local church. It closed: "We recommend that in the meantime all churches within the Convention refrain from taking action on this matter until after the Convention of 1930 has dealt with the

---

12. MacLeod, ed., *Baptist Year Book for Ontario, Quebec and Western Canada, 1929*, 56–57.
13. MacLeod, ed., *Baptist Year Book for Ontario, Quebec and Western Canada, 1929*, 69.

said Commission's report."[14] While this closing sentence—and the resolution as a whole—seemed to suggest that the move toward women's ordination was both inevitable and imminent, it was likely just a reflection of the plan to restructure the ordination process. The resolution passed, and the stage was set to consider the convention's proposal.

Even though women's ordination was obviously a provocative topic, the denominational press, *The Canadian Baptist*, was notably silent on the resolution and its ramifications. Outside of the occasional comment within the newspaper about the work of female missionaries being "precious beyond all estimate,"[15] the closest the newspaper came to weighing in on the debate was its comments on the ordination council itself; yet the question of women's ordination did not seem to come into play in criticisms of this group.[16]

The decision to remain silent on the topic is a curious one; however, there are a few possible reasons for this omission. First, it should be remembered that the convention had only recently emerged from the fundamentalist-modernist controversy, which was a significant theological crisis that wreaked havoc on denominational unity and saw the expulsion or exodus of seventy-seven churches.[17] Opening the ordination process to women might be considered a "liberal" shibboleth, which the denomination's critics could use to justify its attacks and even pursue legal action.[18] Second, limited exposure in the press may reflect the

14. MacLeod, ed., *Baptist Year Book for Ontario, Quebec and Western Canada, 1929*, 54, 68.

15. C. J. Cameron, "The Woman Missionary," *The Canadian Baptist* (22 August 1929), 6.

16. "Three Problems for Churches to Solve," *The Canadian Baptist* (24 April 1930), 15.

17. For more on this controversy, see Adams, "War of the Worlds"; and Adams, "Great Contention." For a study that looks at the role women played in the Baptist fundamentalist community in Ontario during these years, see Murray, "Call."

18. At the time, due to the Baptist principle of the independence of the local congregation, the BCOQ faced legal issues over the ownership of some of its churches and properties, most notably Hughson Street Baptist Church in Hamilton, Ontario. If the convention advocated for a contentious theological

reality that it was an incidental point in the larger conversation on the ordination council itself. By forming a standing council and giving it authority over who would be approved for ordination, the BCOQ was effectively removing a responsibility typically left to the discretion of the local church and giving it to the larger convention body. The resolution's plea to the individual churches, then, reflected the proposed shift in the equilibrium of power: from church to convention. While women's ordination was most certainly a point of discussion within some churches, the conversation on women's ordination during this time may not have resulted from impassioned activists seeking change in the convention and instead was a symptom of the larger conversation.

Due to the limited discussion of the ordination of women in the press, it is difficult to know the environment in which the "Special Committee on the Ordination of Women" found itself heading into the annual convention gathering of 1930. With the Baptists assembled, R. R. McKay, chair of the special committee, presented their findings. Prefacing his comments with the fact that there was no clear precedent for ordaining women among other denominations in Canada and that it had not been practiced by any known Baptist groups, he presented a report that read,

> while recognizing that women are doing an unspeakably valuable work as Sunday School teachers, district visitors, settlement workers, deaconesses, Bible women, missionaries, etc., and while not presuming to circumscribe definitely the religious activities of women, nor from exegesis of Scriptures relevant, to the equality of all believers and kindred subjects to give particularized applications, regarding the restrictions on women's speaking in 1 Corinthians as being occa-

position, their opponents could hypothetically argue that they were not truly Baptist. This was the tactic of fundamentalists in Nova Scotia only a few years later. See Murray, "Exodus to Exile"; and Murray, "From United Baptist to Independent Baptist." In 1947, when the BCOQ did move forward with the ordination of Muriel Spurgeon, fundamentalist Baptists responded characteristically. Put simply: it was further evidence that the convention had apostatized. For a representative example, see "Convention Approves Ordination of Women," *The Gospel Witness* (19 June 1947), 3.

sioned by the social and religious condition of women generally in Corinth and by the apostle's anxiety for the preservation of existing domestic relationships rather than from a wish to suppress women prophets, your Committee does not think that there is. either demand or need, especially at the present time, for beginning a practice which is so entirely new to us as a people.[19]

While the denominational minutes do not record the conversation that followed, it is noteworthy that one Convention pastor, John Galt from Oshawa, immediately added an amendment:

> Whereas; for four hundred years Baptists have consistently recognized and taught the equality of all believers and have never questioned the right of women to take active part in the work and worship of the Church; and whereas Baptists have freely appointed women to represent the Churches at Associations and at Conventions; and whereas Baptists have sent women forth to preach the Gospel to the heath; to teach Christian Doctrine and to have the oversight of churches; and whereas these women messengers faced every difficulty; endured ever hardship and dare every danger equally with men; and whereas the Holy Scripture clearly shows that it pleased God to call women to prophetic office both under law and under grace as instance under Miriam; Deborah; Huldah; Anna; and four daughters of Philip the Evangelist; therefore: be it resolved that the Convention express its approval of the ordination of women on equal terms with men; that is to say, in instances in which there is full proof that God has called them to the work of the Gospel Ministry.[20]

One report from the Convention gathering noted that this amendment sparked an "extended discussion on this important question."[21] Ultimately, however, the amendment was defeated, and the convention delegates adopted the committee's report as presented: women would not be ordained as there was no "need" to do so (the wording of the resolution—namely that the committee believed there was no "need" for women ministers—is ironic,

---

19. MacLeod, ed., *Baptist Year Book for Ontario, Quebec and Western Canada, 1930*, 252.
20. MacLeod, ed., *Baptist Year Book for Ontario, Quebec and Western Canada, 1930*, 42–43.
21. "The Baptist Convention for Ontario and Quebec: James St. Baptist Church, Hamilton," *The Canadian Baptist* (30 October 1930), 4.

given the fact that *The Canadian Baptist* had printed an article just one week ahead of the convention gathering about the "great need" for more Baptist ministers[22]).

Although ordained ministry was closed to them for the time being, women made several other strides within the denomination in the years that followed this discussion. In October 1935, the convention elected its first woman to the council executive as Vice President, Maud Matthews, the abovementioned former member of the special committee on women's ordination.[23] At this same convention, Mrs. J. Hooper argued that since women served as delegates, they should be placed on its board and committees; the delegates responded by electing two women to the resolutions committee.[24] Moreover, that year, Baptists in the region entered into a discussion on the idea of women serving as deacons; one impassioned letter to the editor published in *The Canadian Baptist* suggested, however, that this should have long ceased being an issue at all, and urged churches not to exclude gifted people from any form of leadership.[25]

The First Woman Ordained

The BCOQ suspended the question on women's ordination for the remainder of the 1930s and did not earnestly address it again until the middle of the next decade when, in 1944, Muriel Spurgeon came before the credentials committee to express her

22. "Men for the Ministry," *The Canadian Baptist* (23 October 1930), 3.
23. "First Woman Vice President," *The Canadian Baptist* (31 October 1935), 3.
24. MacLeod, ed., *Baptist Year Book for Ontario, Quebec and Western Canada, 1935*, 31. Unfortunately, we have been unable to locate Ms. Hooper's first name, therefore, we have retained the traditional usage of "Mrs."
25. Marjorie Anderson, "Editor's Mailbag," *The Canadian Baptist* (21 February 1935), 15. Baptist polity generally meant that the question of women serving in the diaconate was left to the discretion of each individual congregation. For a good example of the wide range of perspectives, note the difference between First Cornwallis Baptist Church in Nova Scotia and Brunswick Street Baptist Church in New Brunswick, which first accepted women as deacons in 1919 and 2010, respectively. See Lohnes, "First Cornwallis Baptist Church"; and Atkinson, "Brunswick Street Baptist Church."

interest in pursuing a Bachelor of Divinity degree with the intention of seeking ordination.[26] On one level, ordination seemed like the next natural step in the expanding place of women in Canadian Christianity; however, complicating this question was a trend toward the renewal of traditional gender roles in North American society in the mid-twentieth century—a process that some historians have identified as the "return to domesticity."[27] Following the Second World War, society and the media placed increasing emphasis on family life, and there was a marked return to traditional perspectives on gender. Women married sooner, had children at younger ages, and were less likely to seek higher education and careers. Spurgeon did not fit this mould. Born in England on 1 November 1922, she was a distant relative of the famous English Baptist "Prince of Preachers," Charles Spurgeon.[28] After settling in Canada with her family, she enrolled at McMaster University in Hamilton, Ontario, the BCOQ's traditional training ground, where she received a Bachelor of Arts in Greek and Latin in 1944. By all accounts, she was a bright and assertive woman with a strong personality. In the words of a reporter from *The Toronto Star*, she was also "tolerant and less conservative than many of her fellow Baptists."[29]

As Spurgeon approached the final year of her Bachelor of Divinity degree at McMaster, the topic again came to the forefront. In the denominational records for 1946–1947, the "Report of the Advisory Council on Ministerial Training, Ordinations, Credentials and Discipline" wrote of the special concern that had come before them regarding women students preparing for min-

---

26. At the time of writing, there is no scholarly biography on Spurgeon (later Spurgeon Carder). For biographical information, see Fox, "The Heart and Soul of Mis-sion in India," Canadian Baptist Archives (hereafter CBA), 8.
27. E.g., Stephen, *Pick One Intelligent Girl*, 163–204. For an influential work from the period that diagnosed this trend, see Friedan, *Feminine Mystique*, 15–32.
28. Brackney (*Baptists in North America*, 152) makes this observation, though the exact nature of how they were related is unclear. The same claim is found in "Miss Muriel Spurgeon," *The Canadian Baptist* (1 November 1947), 11.
29. "Miss Spurgeon Described," *The Toronto Star* (14 June 1947).

istry. When presented to the larger convention body, one report from the press noted that it resulted in a "fine-spirited discussion," before adding that the majority in attendance were in favour of moving ahead with women's ordination "provided that these candidates fulfil the highest standards now required of men."[30] As a result, the council recommended that the BCOQ establish a special committee for the admission of women and maintained that the group should also authorize women missionaries (instead of the Home Missions Board, which had previously been the case).[31] This proposal was significant, as it meant women would have to undergo the same credentialing process as men, even to serve as missionaries.

One year later, in 1947, Spurgeon became the first woman to undergo this process. As she was the first woman to approach the ordination council seriously, the group developed what would be a precedent-setting policy in their decision about her. They declared,

> We as a council inline to view that so far as the ordination is a matter of theory, there is not sufficient ground, in the New Testament evidence or Christian conviction, to deny the ordination of women who are properly qualified on the ground of (1) character, (2) inner call, (3) formal training, (4) willingness of Christian company to accept pastoral oversight at their hands.[32]

The council's decision to characterize the debate as "a matter of theory" is an interesting one. Talking of ordination as "theory" was not uncommon among Baptists, and the BCOQ occasionally used it to refer to the concept itself.[33] That said, given this particular context, it is possible that it carried something of a double meaning: women had never been admitted to the ordination process in the past, so, in the council's eyes, it was perhaps still a

---

30. "59th Annual Convention," *The Canadian Baptist* (1 July 1947), 10.
31. Bingham, ed., *Canadian Baptist Yearbook*, 202.
32. Advisory Council on Ordinations, Credentials and Discipline, "Report of the Advisory Council," CBA.
33. For example, see "The Baptist Position," *The Canadian Baptist* (15 May 1947), 9.

theoretical question, which further gives the impression that they approached the decision as an academic exercise.

The council's decision sparked an hour-long debate from which we can glean several interesting details. First, it is noteworthy that no women took part in the discussion. In contrast to the earlier committee to discuss women's ordination in 1929–1930—which included two women—this reality was a corollary of the fact that no women sat on the ordination council, which, given that to date no woman had been ordained, was not necessarily surprising. Second, those present were kept from knowing Spurgeon's identity to avoid prejudice toward the topic based on her character. Of particular concern was Spurgeon's views on dances that had taken place at McMaster. One report circulated in the press at the time noted that Spurgeon had stated: "You talk about young people going wrong because they dance. I believe many more young people go wrong because their parents will not let them go to dances," before continuing, "All they can do then is park and pet. We are not allowed to have liquor at the dances here."[34] Thus, keeping the candidate's identity anonymous came out of a desire to safeguard the integrity of the process.

A third interesting point about the discussion was that the substance of the debate was not built on scriptural principles.[35] According to one report, during the meeting, "no one had gone to the Scriptures."[36] Instead, those who were antagonistic toward women's ordination in part based their criticism on other requirements of the job, including the fact that a woman would not be physically strong enough to perform the ordinance of baptism. When asked why a woman could not perform baptisms, A. J. Vining, council member and well-known denominational official, replied:

---

34. As quoted in "Miss Muriel Spurgeon," *The Gospel Witness* (19 June 1947), 3.

35. Ross Harkness, "Rev. Muriel Spurgeon Sure She Can Baptize Men," *Hamilton Star* (14 June 1947).

36. "Convention Approves Ordination of Women," *The Gospel Witness*, (19 June 1947), 3.

Because she couldn't. Because she doesn't know how. I've known some men to make a mess of baptism and a woman would make a bigger mess of it. I've known men to splash the water around. It's too solemn and beautiful a thing to let women make a mess of it.[37]

To this, C. R. Duncan, fellow council member, retorted:

The only argument against this is the one that rose in my own heart and that I silenced long ago. It is this: I don't like the idea of a woman being my minister or pastor. That argument has no validity. It is just a prejudice. Probably not many churches will want a woman pastor . . . Well let them, but that is prejudice. Even if we ordain woman, those who do not want a woman minister will not have to have one. If it doesn't work out, we can depend on the wisdom of our women not to seek ordination.[38]

Interestingly, his statement about churches not hiring a woman minister if they did not want one proved quite prescient, as will be illustrated later. Although one council member asked for a year to defer the debate, the motion was defeated, and the report passed with a large majority. Spurgeon then assured reporters that she was confident of her ability to baptize a male adult, as she had heard that the weight of a man in the baptismal water was only 35 pounds![39]

Although the examining council had set a precedent for women's ordination, the notion of congregational independence enshrined in Baptist polity meant that the final decision to ordain Spurgeon rested with her own church. On 16 September 1947, Spurgeon attended her examination council at King Street Baptist Church in Kitchener. She attended the meeting feeling confident, believing, "If God wants this, it will happen; If God

---

37. As quoted in Ross Harkness, "Rev. Muriel Spurgeon Sure She Can Baptize Men," *Hamilton Star* (14 June 1947).
38. As quoted in Ross Harkness, "Rev. Muriel Spurgeon Sure She Can Baptize Men," *Hamilton Star* (14 June 1947).
39. Ross Harkness, "Rev. Muriel Spurgeon Sure She Can Baptize Men," *Hamilton Star* (14 June 1947).

doesn't want this, it won't."[40] The vote passed, and the church held a service of ordination that same evening. H. S. Stewart, the Dean of McMaster's Department of Theology, recommended her to the mission board, saying he felt confident she would make an excellent minister. A month after her ordination, Spurgeon sailed for India, where she spent much of her career.[41]

Again, references to this landmark event in both the denominational record and press were surprisingly muted. In the "Report from the Advisory Council," the *Yearbook* quietly reported Spurgeon's ordination and added her name to its list of ministers.[42] *The Link and Visitor*—the primary organ of the Baptist women's missionary board—and *The Canadian Baptist* carried articles that reported news of her ordination and celebrated their first ordained woman but made little comment on the profundity of the decision.[43] Furthermore, there was little apparent response from the public in letters to the editor or other columns responding to Spurgeon's new position. Yet, silence did not equate acceptance, and the lack of opposition in the minutes or the press did not mean the cause of women's ordination had come to a close with a happy ending for those in favour of women's ordination in the BCOQ.

A Second Ordination

After Spurgeon, the BCOQ did not ordain another woman for another 32 years.[44] On 20 October 1979, *The Toronto Star* re-

---

40. Fox, "The Heart and Soul of Mission in India," CBA, 8. This perspective governed Spurgeon's view of ministry. See Muriel Spurgeon, "My Call to Missionary Service," *The Canadian Baptist* (15 July 1947), 9.

41. Details in this paragraph are found in Roy and Watts, "Report on the Working Group on Equality in Ministry," CBA, 3. For another brief resource on Spurgeon's ordination and ministry afterwards, see Barnes, *Our Heritage*, 164–65.

42. Bingham, ed., *Canadian Baptist Yearbook*, 202.

43. E.g., "Miss Muriel Spurgeon," *The Canadian Baptist* (1 November 1947), 11.

44. See "Claire Holmes Ordained in Kingsway," *The Link and Visitor*, (December 1979), 12.

ported that Kingsway Baptist Church, Toronto, "broke new ground" by ordaining the first woman in the BCOQ in over three decades.[45] Born in Hamilton, Ontario, in 1952, Claire Holmes attended McMaster University and was ordained as Associate Pastor of Kingsway Baptist. By this time, Spurgeon Carder—her married name—had returned to Canada, but was serving as a chaplain, which made Holmes the only ordained woman serving in a pastoral office in either Ontario or Quebec. Furthermore, she was one of only five Baptist women ordained in all of Canada, and one of only three serving in a pastoral position.[46] In response to the length of time between the ordinations of Spurgeon Carder and Holmes, the president of the BCOQ quipped: "It takes a while for people's hearts to catch up with their heads," implying that church attitudes had simply not "caught up" to denominational policy until this point.[47] He further conceded that many of the women in training at the time would have difficulty finding placements in churches, as people continued to struggle with the idea of a woman pastoring a church. He said, "Church leadership is keen on that, but, out in the churches, people's attitudes change more slowly."[48]

The time between Spurgeon Carder's ordination and that of Holmes was not lost on the former. Spurgeon Carder took part in the ordination service and gave her own opinion on why three decades had passed: "It was partly due to the climate of opinion, but also to the fact that the Baptist Church is better at making theoretical decisions than carrying them out. Added to this was the fact that I went to India and so was not visible as a woman."[49] Her assessment echoed the ordination council's perspec-

---

45. Tom Harpur, "Baptist Minister is a Rarity, But She is No Women's Libber," *Toronto Star* (20 October 1979), H6.
46. Tom Harpur, "Baptist Minister is a Rarity, But She is No Women's Libber," *Toronto Star* (20 October 1979), H6.
47. Tom Harpur, "Baptist Minister is a Rarity, But She is No Women's Libber," *Toronto Star* (20 October 1979), H6.
48. Tom Harpur, "Baptist Minister is a Rarity, But She is No Women's Libber," *Toronto Star* (20 October 1979), H6.
49. As quoted in Tom Harpur, "Baptist Minister is a Rarity, But She is No Women's Libber," *Toronto Star* (20 October 1979), H6.

tive that the debate over her ordination was really "a matter of theory." The fact that she left Canada shortly after becoming ordained, Spurgeon Carder noted, essentially meant that it remained a theoretical question even after she had been accepted for ordination.

Unlike the cultural context in which Spurgeon Carder had been ordained, the increased role of women in public life was also becoming more normal. When one considers why a renewed interest in women's ordination occurred during the 1970s, it seems reasonably clear to suggest that the women's movement had some part to play in a revived interest in women's careers, and their equality in various professions. This was visible in many other denominations in Canada at the time. In 1975, for example, the Anglican Church was part of an ongoing debate about women ministers, which plateaued when female members vocally considered a lawsuit against the church for discrimination based on the church's unwillingness to ordain women as priests. Similarly, although the United Church had ordained women for several years, it was reported that there was "an unhappy gap between the ideal and the reality," as no woman had held a senior position in a prestigious church until 1975.[50] The Presbyterian Church had opened the ordination process to women in 1966 (although the first woman was not ordained until 1978), while the Pentecostal Church of Canada still did not consider women for ordination.

That more denominations were grappling with the issue is visible in the various debates that occupied other Baptist bodies during the 1970s and 1980s.[51] Most prominently, this era was the beginning of what various observers have called the "conservative resurgence" in the Southern Baptist Convention (SBC). Discussion on the role of women in the church had been prompted by the pronounced place feminism had occupied in the cultural milieu since the 1960s. By 1979, the SBC was locked in a bitter

---

50. Sheila Kieran, "Are Women More Equal in the Church?" *Chatelaine*, (March 1975), 76.

51. This was true of many Evangelical bodies. See Blumhofer, "Confused Legacy," 60.

conflict over the denomination's future, and one of the core issues was "the woman question."[52] While the BCOQ did not experience the same degree of bitter division over this issue,[53] the controversy from the SBC (the largest Baptist body in the world) soon spilled into other, smaller Baptist denominations, who began to grapple with it as well.[54] In *The Canadian Baptist* May 1979 issue, for example, an article bemoaned the lack of women serving in congregations in light of the denomination's official policy of ordaining women. It read: "There is nothing in our theology of the church which says that some members can be 'ordained,' and others can not . . . Our practice, of course, does not correspond to our ecclesiology."[55] The author then went on to state: "If [women] are forced out of the ministry, or out of our Baptist family, they will suffer a grave injustice for which we will all bear some of the responsibility."[56] Respondents to this article challenged its claim based on scriptural grounds.[57] The passion of this discussion might make it seem as if this was the first time the BCOQ had confronted the issue of women's ordination, even though the denomination had been "officially" ordaining women for over thirty years.

To address the remaining theological and cultural concerns that served as a barrier to women's ordination, in 1978, the

---

52. Flowers, *Into the Pulpit*.
53. E.g., An independent national survey of Baptist ministers from 1979 showed that 60 percent of ordained Baptist pastors in the BCOQ believed that the ordination of women had biblical support and therefore also supported it, and 12 percent believed the New Testament was against it, but they still supported it. This was compared to 28 percent who did not believe there was scriptural support and therefore opposed it (see Beverley, "National Survey," 275).
54. Melody Maxwell has documented the significant discussions as they took place among Baptists in Atlantic Canada, who made particularly effective use of their denominational press. See Maxwell, "Proceed with Care"; and Maxwell, "'You Can't, 'Cause You're a Girl.'"
55. G. G. Harrop, "A New Duty for a New Occasion," *The Canadian Baptist* (May 1979), 8–9.
56. G. G. Harrop, "A New Duty for a New Occasion," *The Canadian Baptist* (May 1979), 8–9.
57. E.g., David J. McKinley, "Letter to the Editor," *The Canadian Baptist* (September 1979), 8.

BCOQ developed a "Task Force on Women in Ministry." The task force consisted of thirteen individuals (seven regularly elected members and five *ex-officio* members). Among the regularly elected members were Holmes and Spurgeon Carder.[58] Its stated purpose was to research the current status of women in ministry and to develop policies to promote the use of women in ministry in the congregations. In one of its earliest meetings, the task force agreed that "the greatest hurdle to full acceptance of Women in Ministry relates to the attitudinal response of the people in the local congregation."[59] Citing the need for research on "both sides" of the position, they suggested an emphasis on Bible study, a review of cultural expectations, and a reassessment of the recruitment, training, and support of students coming into ministry in light of the needs and the kind of employment available to them.[60] Their final report eventually called for renewed education and teaching in churches to encourage positive attitudes towards women in ministry.[61]

Conclusion

The preceding narrative exposes several factors in the disconnect between official policy and denominational practice. As noted by Spurgeon Carder herself, since she was ordained as a missionary, it kept the denomination from dealing with women ministers in their "regular" congregations. Her plans for the ministry made her a relatively innocuous first female candidate for ordination.

58. The other members were Murray J. S. Ford (Chair), Fanshun Watts, John Coutts, Glen Barrett, George Scott, Audrey Manuel, Ron Watts, Ken Morrison, H. Lewis, and L. V. Hultgren (Meeting of the BCOQ Department of the Ministry, Thursday, 27 March 1980, CBA, 87).

59. Ford, "Task Force on Women in Ministry: Minutes" (5 June 1978), CBA. Likewise, in late 1979, they noted that "the greatest task is that of educating our churches that they give equal consideration to women candidates" (Meeting of the BCOQ Department of the Ministry, Thursday, 1 November 1979, CBA, 87).

60. Ford, "Task Force on Women in Ministry: Minutes," 5 June 1978, CBA.

61. Ford, "Report to the Department of the Ministry on Behalf of the Task Force on Women in Ministry," n.d., CBA.

The fact that the denominational press dealt with her case so sparingly would seem to indicate that the event was of little genuine consequence for the life of the convention, even though it was a historic and monumental decision. Moreover, one must consider the attitudes of the individual churches. As A. C. Duncan stated during the debate over ordination in 1947, due to Baptist polity, churches did not have to ordain someone that they did not wish to ordain.[62] Therefore, whatever public policy may have been, it is evident that the attitudes of individual churches played a significant role in Baptist circles regarding whether or not a woman found a place to be ordained. It was not until the cultural and religious setting had sufficiently changed that the BCOQ tangibly ratified its decision to ordain women to ministry. These observations show that the BCOQ was much more reluctant to accept women's ordination than historians commonly recognize.

Attitudes on women's ordination have changed since the early twentieth century, and while it remains a sensitive topic for some, it has lost some of its stigma. Notably, in 2023, the Canadian Baptists of Ontario and Quebec (CBOQ; formerly the BCOQ) appointed a woman—with unanimous approval—to the position of Executive Minister for the first time in Canadian Baptist history. At the same time, although the number of women ministers has increased in the CBOQ since the period under review, the ordained ministry remains largely male-dominated. Today, with the precedents of women like Spurgeon Carder and Holmes, it is likely that the greatest barrier is the continued congregational attitudes towards women in ministry. Indeed, even for churches that support women in ministry, many remain reluctant to call a woman to their own congregation. It is not the purpose of this paper to diagnose the state of Baptist churches today; however, it may serve to provide a historical backdrop for these kinds of conversations.

---

62. Duncan quote from Ross Harkness, "Rev. Muriel Spurgeon Sure She Can Baptize Men," *Hamilton Star* (14 June 1947).

Bibliography

Adams, Doug. "The Great Contention: Ontario Baptists and the Fundamentalist-Modernist Struggle for McMaster University, 1919–1927." In *Canadian Baptist Fundamentalism, 1878–1978*, edited by Taylor Murray and Paul R. Wilson, 119–56. McMaster General Studies 14. Canadian Baptist History Society Series 4. Eugene, OR: Pickwick, 2022.

———. "The War of the Worlds: The Militant Fundamentalism of Dr. Thomas Todhunter Shields and the Paradox of Modernity." PhD diss., University of Western Ontario, 2015.

Atkinson, Terry. "Brunswick Street Baptist Church." In *Maritime Baptist Old First Churches: Narratives and Prospects*, edited by William H. Brackney with Evan Colford, 119–35. Wolfville, NS: ACBAS and the Editorial Committee of the Canadian Baptists of Atlantic Canada Historical Committee, 2017.

Barnes, Esther. *Our Heritage Becomes our Challenge: A Scrapbook History of the Baptist Women's Movement in Ontario and Quebec*. Etobicoke, ON: Canadian Baptist Women of Ontario and Quebec, 2013.

Beverley, James A. "National Survey of Baptist Ministers." In *Baptists in Canada: Search for Identity Amidst Diversity*, edited by Jarold K. Zeman, 267–76. Burlington, ON: Welch, 1980.

Bingham, H. H., ed. *Canadian Baptist Yearbook, 1946–47*. Toronto: Standard, 1947.

Blumhofer, Edith L. "A Confused Legacy: Reflections of Evangelical Attitudes toward Ministering Women in the Past Century." *Fides et Historia* 22 (1990) 49–61.

Brackney, William H. *Baptists in North America*. Religious Life in America 2. Malden, MA: Blackwell, 2006.

Brouwer, Ruth Compton. *New Women for God: Canadian Presbyterian Women and India Missions, 1876–1914*. Toronto: University of Toronto Press, 1990.

The Canadian Baptist, 1893, 1929, 1930, 1935, 1947, 1979.

Canadian Baptist Archives, McMaster University, Hamilton, ON.

Chatelaine, 1979.

Chaves, Mark. *Ordaining Women: Culture and Conflict in Religious Organizations*. Cambridge, MA: Harvard University Press, 1999.

Colwell, Judith. "The Role of Women in Nineteenth-Century Church of Ontario." *Canadian Society of Church History Papers* (1985) 31–57.

Cook, Sharon Anne. *"Through Sunshine and Shadow": The Woman's Christian Temperance Union, Evangelicalism, and Reform in Ontario, 1874–1930*. McGill-Queen's Studies in the History of Religion 1/19. Kingston: McGill-Queen's University Press, 1995.

Flowers, Elizabeth H. *Into the Pulpit: Southern Baptist Women and Power Since World War II*. Chapel Hill: University of North Carolina Press, 2012.

Friedan, Betty. *The Feminine Mystique*. New York: Norton, 1963.

Gagan, Rosemary R. *A Sensitive Independence: Canadian Methodist Women Missionaries in Canada and the Orient, 1881–1925*. McGill-Queen's Studies in the History of Religion 1/9. Kingston: McGill-Queen's University Press, 1992.

Gospel Witness, 1947.

Hamilton Star, 1947.

Heath, Gordon L., Dallas Friesen, and Taylor Murray. *Baptists in Canada: Their History and Polity*. McMaster Ministry Studies Series 5. Eugene, OR: Pickwick, 2020.

Korinek, Valerie J. "No Women Need Apply: The Ordination of Women in the United Church, 1918–1965." *Canadian Historical Review* 74 (1993) 473–509.

Link and Visitor, 1979.

Lohnes, Peter. "First Cornwallis Baptist Church." In *Maritime Baptist Old First Churches: Narratives and Prospects*, edited by William H. Brackney with Evan Colford, 137–64. Wolfville, NS: ACBAS and the Editorial Committee of the Canadian Baptists of Atlantic Canada Historical Committee, 2017.

MacLeod, C. E., ed. *Baptist Year Book for Ontario, Quebec and Western Canada, 1929*. Toronto: Standard, 1929.

———, ed. *Baptist Year Book for Ontario, Quebec and Western Canada, 1930*. Toronto: Standard, 1930.

———, ed. *Baptist Year Book for Ontario, Quebec and Western Canada, 1935*. Toronto: Standard, 1935.

Maxwell, Melody. "'Proceed with Care': Atlantic Baptists and Women's Ordination in the 1980s." *Baptist History and Heritage* 55 (2020) 52–69.

———. "'You Can't, 'Cause You're a Girl': Atlantic Baptist Women Navigating Call, Ordination, and Opposition, 1976–1987." *McMaster Journal of Theology and Ministry* 22 (2020–2021) 61–82.

Mullen, Vesta Dunlop. *"I Believe in the Communion of Saints": Ordained Ministers of the Reformed Baptist Church, 1888–1966*. Old Shoals, IN: Old Paths Tract Society, 2006.

Murray, Taylor. "'A Call to [Fundamentalist] Baptist Women': Caroline Holman and the Women's Missionary Society of the Regular Baptists of Canada, 1926–1933." PhD diss., McMaster Divinity College, 2023.

———. "Exodus to Exile: Independent Baptists in Nova Scotia, 1934–1939." *American Baptist Quarterly* 37 (2017) 282–303.

———. "From United Baptist to Independent Baptist: Fundamentalism and Baptist Identity in the Maritime Provinces of Canada in the 1930s." In *Canadian Baptist Fundamentalism, 1878–1978*, edited by Taylor Murray and Paul R. Wilson, 179–204. McMaster General Studies 14. Canadian Baptist Historical Society Series 4. Eugene, OR: Pickwick, 2022.

Reid-Maroney, Nina. *The Reverend Jennie Johnson and African Canadian History, 1868–1967*. Rochester, NY: University of Rochester Press, 2013.

Renfree, Harry. *Heritage and Horizon: The Baptist Story in Canada*. Mississauga, ON: Canadian Baptist Federation, 1988.

Stephen, Jennifer Anne. *Pick One Intelligent Girl: Employability, Domesticity and the Gendering of Canada's Welfare*

State, 1939–1947. Toronto: University of Toronto Press, 2007.

Strong-Boag, Veronica. *"Janey Canuck": Women in Canada, 1919–1939*. Historical Booklet 53. Ottawa: Canadian Historical Association, 1994.

Toronto Star, 1947, 1979.

Whiteley, Marilyn Färdig. *Canadian Methodist Women, 1766–1925: Marys, Marthas, Mothers in Israel*. Studies in Women and Religion 10. Waterloo, ON: Wilfrid Laurier University Press, 2005.

THE VALUE OF PRAISE: *PRIDE AND PREJUDICE* AS A PORTRAIT OF WHO WE ARE AS WORSHIPPERS

D. S. Martin
Poet-in-Residence, McMaster Divinity College, Hamilton, ON

Although we all love to receive compliments, not all compliments are worth receiving. The source of the compliment matters. It matters if the person is discerning, honest, and not trying to extract a favour from you. It matters if the person knows what they are talking about. If a great singer were to praise your voice it would mean more than if your tone-deaf mother did.

When someone you esteem as a person of great discernment praises your skills in a field they know well, you appreciate it far more than if it were from someone insincere, less knowledgeable about the field, or even someone just trying to be nice. If someone who truly knows you compliments your character, it means more than if a stranger were to say it.

Praise that is steeped in truth and sincerity is the only praise that really matters. This is why Jesus says that it is worshippers who worship in Spirit and truth that the Father seeks.

These thoughts arose for me in a different sort of way as I read Jane Austen's novel *Pride and Prejudice* (1813). The novel is a masterwork of character study—particularly related to people who are ready to make pronouncements about others and those whose traits are misunderstood. If all the characters from the novel were to gather in the same church and sing hymns of praise to our God, which ones would be worthy worshippers? Where might you fit, in comparison with them, and what might you do, by the power of the Holy Spirit, to become a more fit worshipper?

Many of these people would need to undergo a significant transformation before being able to bring true worship (whether in song or in silence) to God. Although in some ways at opposite ends of the spectrum, the manipulator and womanizer Wickham, and the arrogant aristocrat Lady Catherine de Bourgh—neither are ready to prioritize anyone but themselves. Our worship, if we have such attitudes, is only external playacting.

Jane Austen clearly believed when she wrote *Pride and Prejudice* that we are as honest as we allow ourselves to be, that we are able to improve our skills of discernment and we can learn from our own foolish mistakes. If you have recently read the novel, or seen the film (2005), or viewed the visually stunning five-and-a-half-hour BBC miniseries (1995), you will recognize much from my portraits of Austen's characters and be able to thoughtfully consider each one.

Every member of the Bennet family, whom we are introduced to right from the start, expresses their opinions of others, as does every character in the book. Elizabeth's mother is only ready to praise those she wants something from—particularly rich and handsome young men she would like to have marry one of her daughters. She is dishonest, perhaps even with herself, when she speaks of the character of such young men, since her assessments have little to do with their behaviour, and her pronouncements change even when behaviour does not. Any praise for God coming from Mrs. Bennet's lips would have to do with whether God gave her what she wanted or not.

The obsession of the youngest sisters is to flirt with whatever handsome young man in a soldier's uniform comes into view—regardless of his character. In a field of wildflowers, or a church service, they would have no thoughts for worship. Even the virtuous eldest daughter Jane has no sense of discernment; she seems incapable of finding fault in anyone, and therefore any praise from her would be shallow. In a contest when no one loses, no one wins. If Jane Bennet were to say you are kind or intelligent or talented, it would mean nothing because to her everyone is. Would words of praise from any of these girls mean very much?

Like so many of these characters, we all fall short of being worthy worshippers—and yet we are encouraged to make the effort. In Ps 100, as in other psalms, we are instructed to,

> Worship the LORD with gladness;
> come before him with joyful songs.

The psalm also directs us to know him for who he is and for what he has done. This is where our praise springs from.

You might expect that the clergyman Mr. Collins would be most fit for worshipping God. He certainly must be a student of Scripture and has developed eloquence of speech. Collins's character, however, has been formed through his attempts to curry favour. He is insincere, cringing before his benefactress with false humility, bragging to others of his connections, and valuing status and comfort above everything. It seems to me that to Collins, religion is merely his line of business and that he is more concerned with what Lady Catherine de Bourgh thinks, than with what God thinks.

In a novel such as *Pride and Prejudice* that is so much about people who are biased in their assessments of others, we need a protagonist whose judgment is sound. Austen—in her brilliance—has given us Elizabeth Bennet, who is a discerning character from the start, but is also capable of making serious errors in such judgment. What the author does so well, is lead us through Elizabeth's humble reassessment of the prideful prejudice that has influenced her judgment of Wickham's character, and more significantly, of Darcy's.

Elizabeth's errors come from judging based on appearance. When the prophet Samuel is sent to anoint a new king for Israel, God warns him not to make this mistake: "People look at the outward appearance, but the Lord looks at the heart" (1 Sam 16:7, ESV). Elizabeth begins to view Mr. Darcy differently once she starts to get to know him—listening to what those who know him best say about him and learning more about him through his actions. She becomes wise enough to repent of her earlier prejudices, realizing they were not based on truth.

And so, we must consider our own pride and our own prejudices, as barricades to our being the sort of worshippers the Father seeks. We must learn to discern and worship our God based on who he is—not on what we can get out of the deal. We must set our self-interest aside, trusting him even when our most-desperate prayers are met with silence. We must worship him in Spirit and in truth.

Polishing Mirrors for Heaven

Philip Yancey
Evergreen, CO, USA

I have visited Russia twice. The first time, in 1991, I found a nation in deep chaos. The Soviet Union was rapidly disintegrating, and that year's news featured a failed coup against President Mikhail Gorbachev and the resulting power struggle led by Boris Yeltsin. Ultimately, Yeltsin would triumph over Russia's diehard communists, after leading a military attack on the parliament building and introducing a new era of freedom and openness to the West.

On my second visit, in 2002, I traveled to Saint Petersburg to attend a Christian book fair, itself an emblem of the changes that had swept across the country. By then, some 7,000 missionaries had flooded into Russia, whose citizens now confronted a bewildering array of denominations and cults, each of which offered an alternative to the thousand-year traditions of the Russian Orthodox Church.

One afternoon, I toured the renowned Hermitage Museum, spending most of my time in the magnificent gallery devoted to works by Rembrandt. I watched as teachers escorted groups of Russian schoolchildren into the room. They bravely tried to hold the fidgeting kids' attention while describing the various paintings, especially those with religious themes: *David and Jonathan*, *The Holy Family with Angels*, *Descent from the Cross*, *The Sacrifice of Isaac*, and, most prominently, *Return of the Prodigal Son*.

Observing the groups of children, it struck me that despite 75 years of militant atheism—during which 42,000 priests had been killed and 98 percent of churches shuttered—Christianity had never departed from Russia. Icons and paintings, such as those by Rembrandt, kept alive the stories that had long been suppressed, and now ordinary schoolteachers were free to explain their message to a new generation.

Little did I know that Russia's window of religious freedom would soon slam shut. Already a new President, Vladimir Putin, was drafting laws that would result in the expulsion of all missionaries as "foreign agents" and restore the power of Russian Orthodoxy. In return, the Orthodox patriarch would become one of the main cheerleaders supporting the brutal invasions of Ukraine.

In subsequent years, I visited other countries in the former Soviet orbit: Ukraine, Belarus, Kazakhstan, Bulgaria, Hungary, Poland, Czech Republic, Serbia, the three tiny Baltic countries, and Romania. In each of them, I found a small but vibrant Christian community still exulting in the freedom to worship. And in Romania I met a remarkable artist named Liviu Mocan.

Hailing from Transylvania, a region known mainly as the setting for Dracula and other vampires, Mocan has gained international acclaim as a sculptor who brazenly focuses on religious themes. While I was speaking at a pastors' conference, he stood by my side, extemporaneously fashioning sculptures to illustrate what I was saying. Mocan became a dear friend, a larger-than-life artist who specializes in larger-than-life sculptures.

Mocan shatters the stereotype of the reclusive, introverted artist. In a restaurant, his booming voice and infectious spirit often take over the room. I have seen him move from table to table shaking hands and introducing himself to total strangers. One evening, he hosted a banquet for fifty people in his home and somehow talked me into joining a group of Romanian dancers in local costumes.

Yet in his studio and forge, Mocan is all business. Besides the ancient craft of metalworking, he has also incorporated modern techniques such as computer-aided design, 3D printing, and laser cutting.

When Romania held a contest to commemorate the demonstrators who were shot during protests against the dictator Ceausescu in 1989, Mocan's submission, *The Shot Pillars*, won.

The Shot Pillars

It stands in his home city as a memorial to those who helped topple an oppressive regime.

Mocan studied art at a state-sponsored school in the 1970s, when he had to embed his works' meaning in a kind of code. Public expression of Christian faith was a serious crime under Ceausescu's rule in Romania. Now free to express himself openly, Mocan is happy to elucidate the messages and symbolism in his artwork.

One professor described Mocan's work as "reverse dadaism," a kind of antidote to existential despair. In an era when modern art often centers on themes of meaninglessness, violence, and sexuality, Mocan celebrates freedom, joy, and the lasting contributions of the Christian faith. Among his many awards, he received a national prize for *The Heart of Resurrection*. In 2009, Switzerland commissioned him to create a monumental sculpture in Geneva to commemorate the five-hundredth anniversary of John Calvin's birth.

The Book That Reads You (I)

A few years later Mocan made a set of brass sculptures to celebrate the essence of the Protestant Reformation—an ironic homage, since some Reformers had stripped churches of artistic images. The series, titled *Reformation—The Five Solas*, includes these pieces.

- *Sola Scriptura*: by Scripture alone
- *Sola Fide*: by faith alone
- *Sola Gratia*: by grace alone
- *Solus Christus*: through Christ alone
- *Soli Deo Gloria*: for God's glory alone

His series of sculptures on "by Scripture alone" brings new life to the normally boring representation of printed books, especially the Bible. And Mocan takes seriously that last motif "for God's glory alone" as seen in *The Trumpet in the Universe*, now displayed at Wheaton College. God is the true artist, he insists, and we simply try to reflect back some of the beauty that God has lavished on earth. Mocan says about his work,

> I am striving to polish mirrors for heaven . . . When my hands touch the marble or the granite or the wood, when my hands deepen in soft clay, I touch God's hands. God's hands are there waiting for me . . .

This is how, resculpting his sculptures, I understand, day by day, how inadequate I am. I am a sculptor, I am a sculpture.

Mocan's work harks back to a time when the church both inspired and patronized the arts. Great examples have endured despite the sometimes-hostile history taking place around them. He stands in the tradition of Caravaggio, da Vinci, and Michelangelo, as well as Handel, Bach, Dante, and Milton.

In modern Europe and North America, the church is seldom seen as a font of inspiration for the arts. But as I saw in the Hermitage Museum, art can express faith in a durable way even when words are forced to fall silent. Perhaps decades from now Russian schoolchildren will be studying artists like Liviu Mocan as they learn about a faith that decades of atheism—or institutional religion—could not suppress.

AFTERWORD

D. S. Martin
Poet-in-Residence, McMaster Divinity College, Hamilton, ON

"Polishing Mirrors for Heaven," as it stands to this point, is really part one of the story Philip Yancey began and which I have been asked to conclude on his behalf. This second part tells of American poet Jill Peláez Baumgaertner and the book of poems she has created and presented in partnership with Mocan's sculptures, entitled *The Shapes Are Real* (Poiema; Eugene, OR: Cascade, forthcoming [2025]).

Baumgaertner is Professor of English Emerita at Wheaton College, where she served as Dean of Humanities and Theological Studies 2001–2017. The connection began when Dr. Michael Wilder, Dean of Communication and Arts at Wheaton, shared photos with her of some of Mocan's work and expressed the desire to feature one of his sculptures in the lobby outside the concert hall in the newly built Armerding Center for the Arts at Wheaton College.

Baumgaertner and her husband were so taken with Liviu Mocan's sculptures—particularly *Soli Deo Gloria*, which Jill says is magnificent and perfect for the location—that they became the required donors to make this installation possible. Later, they also purchased Mocan's *The Book That Reads You* and eventually placed in the newly designed library.

Baumgaertner told me,

> I got to know Liviu and his wife Rodica when they came for the dedication. We had dinner and lively conversation and, in the process, realized that we had identical, or at least very similar, ideas about the gift of creation that God so generously gives to artists—and the responsibility to praise him through our work and tell his stories and lift percipients to new understandings of his glory. We hatched the idea of collaborating on a book of photos of his sculptures and poems that I would write—not necessarily about the sculptures—but inspired by them.

This was a project she felt was important for her to complete, even though she had no idea whether it was something a publisher would be willing or able to take on. When she shared her poems with me—since I had been the editor for one of her earlier collections, *What Cannot Be Fixed* (Poiema; Eugene, OR: Cascade, 2014)—I could see that her approach to ekphrastic poetry was consistently more about capturing the spirit of the artwork than about merely documenting it.

In the opening stanza of a poem responding to *The Birth of Poetry*, a sculpture Liviu Mocan dedicated to Jill Baumgaertner, she writes,

> Before the words surface,
> before the first breath, they are all
> curls and stabs, floating there,
> porous, delicate as glass yet lethal,
> leaking danger but up up breathing at last
> a limber word that lightly
> brushes the bronze, the gift
> of radical syllables uttered and answered
> before they coalesce.

My eye goes from the poem to the image and back to the poem again. It is as if the sculptor is responding to the poet as much as the poet is responding to the sculptor. In reality, both are responding to the vison they share of how Christian artists of whatever discipline let their God-dominated imaginations speak.

The Birth of Poetry
(Bronze; 125 cm [height]; dedicated to Jill Baumgaertner)

The sculptures, clearly stand on their own, and the poems work independently of the images. Even so, when they are considered together, greater possibilities emerge.

Baumgaertner says, "We want our book to tell the story that begins in radiance and beauty, progressed through sin to the fall, and leads to revelation and redemption through the vast and tender love of Christ." This is exactly what they have accomplished.

I hope this essay now fulfills Philip Yancey's intentions for it—to be more than merely an introduction to a significant Christian sculptor, and more than a preview of Mocan's partnership with Baumgaertner in her new poetry book *The Shapes Are Real* (forthcoming [2025]).

Perhaps we might yet be on the verge of reviving our influence on the culture around us, harkening "back to a time when the church both inspired and patronized the arts."

https://mcmasterdivinity.ca/mjtm/mcmaster-journal-of-theology-and-ministry-volume-twenty-four-2022-2023

Schrock, David S. *The Royal Priesthood and the Glory of God.* Short Studies in Biblical Theology. Wheaton, IL: Crossway, 2022. Reviewed by Ki Hyun Kim.

Walton, John H. *Wisdom for Faithful Reading: Principles and Practices for Old Testament Interpretation.* Downers Grove, IL: InterVarsity, 2023. Reviewed by Phillip D. Haskell.

Köstenberger, Andreas J., and Gregory Goswell. *Biblical Theology: A Canonical, Thematic, and Ethical Approach.* Wheaton, IL: Crossway, 2023. Reviewed by Deven K. MacDonald.

Carr, David M. *Genesis 1–11.* International Exegetical Commentary on the Old Testament. Stuttgart: Kohlhammer, 2021. Reviewed by Dustin Burlet.

Roberto, John, ed. *Digital Ministry and Leadership in Today's Church.* Collegeville, MN: Liturgical, 2022. Reviewed by Wesley B. Sloat.

Allen, Holly Catterton, et al. *Intergenerational Christian Formation: Bringing the Whole Church Together in Ministry, Community, and Worship.* 2nd ed. Downers Grove, IL: IVP Academic, 2023. Reviewed by Carveth DeLeon.

Jervis, L. Ann. *Paul and Time: Life in the Temporality of Christ.* Grand Rapids: Baker Academic, 2023. Reviewed by Yoshihiro Takahashi.

O'Donnell, Karen. *The Dark Womb: Re-Conceiving Theology through Reproductive Loss.* London: SCM, 2022. Reviewed by Tamara L. Simmonds.

Kim-Cragg, HyeRan. *Postcolonial Preaching: Creating a Ripple Effect.* Lanham, MD: Lexington, 2021. Reviewed by David M. Csinos.

Gertz, Jan Christian. *Genesis 1–11*. Historical Commentary on the Old Testament. Leuven: Peeters, 2023. Reviewed by Dustin Burlet.

Hastings, W. Ross. *The Resurrection of Jesus Christ: Exploring its Theological Significance and Ongoing Relevance*. Grand Rapids: Baker Academic, 2022. Reviewed by Ronald Ames Roberts.

Hull, Brian, and Patrick Mays. *Youth Ministry as Mission: A Conversation about Theology and Culture*. Grand Rapids: Kregel Academic, 2022. Reviewed by Grace Tirado.

www.ingramcontent.com/pod-product-compliance
Lightning Source LLC
Chambersburg PA
CBHW050838160426
43192CB00011B/2072